QUESTIONS & ANSWERS:
PROPERTY

QUESTIONS & ANSWERS: PROPERTY

*Multiple Choice and Short Answer
Questions and Answers*

SECOND EDITION

JOHN COPELAND NAGLE
John N. Matthews Professor
University of Notre Dame
The Law School

ISBN: 978-0-7698-6510-2
eBook ISBN: 978-0-3271-8981-7

This publication is designed to provide authoritative information in regard to the subject matter covered. It is sold with the understanding that the publisher is not engaged in rendering legal, accounting, or other professional services. If legal advice or other expert assistance is required, the services of a competent professional should be sought.

> **NOTE TO USERS**
> To ensure that you are using the latest materials available in this area, please be sure to periodically check the LexisNexis Law School web site for downloadable updates and supplements at www.lexisnexis.com/lawschool.

Editorial Offices
121 Chanlon Rd., New Providence, NJ 07974 (908) 464-6800
201 Mission St., San Francisco, CA 94105-1831 (415) 908-3200
www.lexisnexis.com

MATTHEW♦BENDER

(2014–Pub.3178)

Dedication

For Laura and Julia, who are learning what property is really all about.

About the Author

John Copeland Nagle is John N. Matthews Professor at University of Notre Dame, The Law School, where he teaches property, legislation, and a variety of environmental law courses. He is the co-author of "The Law of Biodiversity and Ecosystem Management," the first book designed for courses studying how the law addresses biodiversity. He is also co-authoring a forthcoming property law casebook and a book comparing environmental pollution, cultural pollution, and other kinds of "pollution." He has lectured on property, legislation, and environmental issues at numerous forums in the United States, Canada, China, and Hungary. He served as a Distinguished Lecturer at the Tsinghua University School of Law in Beijing during 2002, where he taught property law and environmental law.

Prior to joining the Notre Dame faculty, Professor Nagle was an associate professor at the Seton Hall University School of Law from 1994 through 1998. He also worked in the United States Department of Justice, first as an attorney in the Office of Legal Counsel where he advised other executive branch agencies on a variety of constitutional and statutory issues, and later as a trial attorney conducting environmental litigation. Professor Nagle served as a law clerk to Judge Deanell Reece Tacha of the United States Court of Appeals for the Tenth Circuit, and he was a scientific assistant in the Energy and Environmental Systems Division of Argonne National Laboratory. He is a graduate of Indiana University and the University of Michigan Law School.

Preface

Property law has a reputation for being the most difficult of the courses encountered in the first year of law school. That reputation is well earned, for the intricacies of such longstanding common law doctrines as the Rule against Perpetuities have confounded generations of law students, lawyers, judges, and professors. But much of property law relies upon the application of contemporary policies to our rapidly developing societies. An effective property law course will teach both the old rules and the new policies. This book is designed to achieve that goal, too.

This book contains questions and answers. Its primary purpose is to help you test your knowledge of the full range of property law concepts and to apply that knowledge to particular situations. Some of those situations are real, as indicated by the cases cited in the answers. Other cases are hypothetical, yet they should illustrate the problems addressed by property law equally well. The questions take two forms: short answer questions and multiple choice questions. Each of the short answer questions is designed to be answered in between five and ten minutes. The multiple choice questions should be answered in about two minutes each. The practice final exam, therefore, should take about 180 minutes to complete. But it is also important to take the time to answer every question as carefully as possible, even if that requires more time than the suggested guidelines. The point, after all, is to test your knowledge of property law, and to identify those areas where further study is needed.

I am grateful to LEXIS for publishing this valuable series of books, to Tim Zinnecker for excellent editorial advice, and to my students who continue to teach me about property law.

Professor John Copeland Nagle
Notre Dame, Indiana
Fall 2013

Table of Contents

QUESTIONS

1. The occupation theory is best illustrated by the law governing which type of property?

    a. Oil & gas.

    b. Surface water in the eastern United States.

    c. Trademarks.

    d. Human body parts.

2. How does cultural property differ from other kinds of property?

ANSWER:

3. Which of the following is an example of a right to use property that does not include the ownership of that property?

    a. Riparian water rights.

    b. Trade secrets.

    c. Adverse possession of personal property.

    d. The rule of capture.

4. In *Willcox v. Stroup*, the Fourth Circuit held that Thomas Willcox was the rightful owner of Civil War letters that he found in his grandmother's attic because property is presumed to be owned by the one who possesses it. The court thus demonstrated which theory of property?

    a. Natural law.

    b. Occupation.

    c. Utilitarian.

    d. Labor.

5. Which of the following is an example of an anticommons?

    a. National forest lands used for livestock grazing.

    b. Land that is zoned for residential use only.

    c. A song written by Miley Cyrus.

    d. Biotechnology inventions with many individual components.

6.   Jeremy Bentham's utilitarian theory of property implies that:

    a. The federal Wilderness Act properly prevents human use of land.

    b. The Visual Artists Rights Act is based upon the improper premise that natural rights determine property.

    c. Local zoning laws are invalid because they rest upon an arbitrary community judgment about how to use property.

    d. Reforms in landlord and tenant law are misguided to the extent that they rely upon contract law principles.

7.   Which property is the law most likely to allow to be destroyed?

    a. A patented machine.

    b. A famous sculpture.

    c. An historic theater.

    d. A pet cat.

8.   Capture is most likely to determine property rights to each of following *except*:

    a. Animals.

    b. Natural gas.

    c. Land created by avulsion.

    d. Groundwater.

9.   The Stratosphere Resort and Casino applied to build a roller coaster ride on Las Vegas Boulevard that would plunge down a 325-foot tower at 93 miles per hour. The city council unanimously refused to approve the necessary zoning change because of neighborhood opposition. Before he voted, Mayor Oscar Goodman explained, "If anyone in the neighborhood feels that this particular project is such that it will destroy their quality of life as they perceive it, then I have to feel that I must support the neighbors against the Stratosphere as far as these issues are concerned." The mayor's statement and decision best illustrate:

    a. The tragedy of the commons.

    b. The tragedy of the anticommons.

    c. The labor theory of property.

    d. The natural rights theory of property.

10. The Visual Artists Rights Act of 1990 illustrates:

    a. The role of natural rights in determining property.

    b. The primary authority of landowners with respect to property.

    c. The constitutional direction that intellectual property rights be of an unlimited duration.

    d. The unwillingness of the law to make judgments about artistic value.

11. The aphorism that "possession is nine-tenths of the law" is best disproved by the law of:

    Avulsion.

    b. Accretion.

    c. Accession.

    d. Adverse possession.

12. Nineteenth-century American statesman Henry Clay once wrote, "That is property which the law declares to be property." Clay's definition best illustrates which theory of property?

ANSWER:

13. Which type of property law provides the least protection to the right to exclude?

    a. The federal trademark act.

    b. State riparian rights to water.

    c. State public accommodations statutes.

    d. Municipal historic preservation ordinances.

14. Which of the following legal doctrines finds the most support from the scriptural indication that landowners should be willing to let others use their land?

    a. Tenancies at sufferance.

    b. The public trust doctrine.

    c. The touch and concern requirement.

    d. Spot zoning prohibitions.

15.   What is the most likely source of a prohibition on a casino's right to exclude a patron who is counting cards at the blackjack table?

ANSWER:

16. Amy gave away all her baby clothes, furniture, car seat, and other infant items to various friends and families. She thought she was finished with having any more kids, but then she discovered that she was unexpectedly pregnant with her eighth child. She worries that it is going to be difficult financially to re-purchase all the things she gave away. What is her best legal argument for recovering all of the infant items?

ANSWER:

17. Norwood purchased 190 heifers at the Valentine livestock auction on March 27, 2008. The next day, Norwood shipped the heifers to Asbury, a cattle breeder with whom he had done business before. Asbury agreed to provide bulls to breed the heifers, pay half of the mineral costs, pay all veterinarian bills for the heifers, and pay half of the veterinarian expenses for the resulting calves. The calves would then be sold at weaning time, with Norwood and Asbury dividing the proceeds equally. Norwood learned the heifers were no longer at Asbury's in October 2008, when law enforcement personnel informed him that Asbury had been foreclosed on by the bank and that there were not "very many cattle left there." According to Norwood, he confronted Asbury, who informed him that because of the foreclosure, he had moved the heifers "to a safe place." According to Asbury, when the heifers left his property, they were delivered to Hargrove, but Asbury confirmed that Norwood did not agree to this. According to Hargrove, he purchased 140 head of bred heifers from Asbury. Hargrove then sold the 140 heifers to Maulsby. Who owns the heifers now?

ANSWER:

18. Numerous file cabinets were purchased from First National Bank of Chicago in June 2011 by Walter Zibton, a new and secondhand office supply and furniture dealer, as part of a group of items sold on an "as is" basis by First Chicago as they were no longer being used. Zibton then put the file cabinets on sale at a parking lot sale in early July 2011. Charles Strayve indicated an interest in one of the file cabinets up for sale and was told by Zibton that he could have it, without paying anything, if he took all four file cabinets left on the lot. Strayve took all four file cabinets and gave one to his friend Richard Michael. About six weeks later, on August 18, 2011, Michael was moving the file cabinet in his garage. It fell over and several of the locked drawers opened revealing over 1,600 certificates of deposit, payable to "bearer" and worth a total of $6,687,948.85. Who has the best legal claim to the certificates of deposit?

ANSWER:

19. Dr. Rebhi Hazen took his laptop computer to Best Buy so that the store could download all of his photo files onto CDs that he planned to buy from the store. A Best Buy employee downloaded the photos but then lost the CDs. Will Hazen's lawsuit against Best Buy for the loss of the CDs succeed?

ANSWER:

20. Treasure trove law is designed to reward those who:

    a. Look for lost treasures.

    b. Own land.

    c. Seek to identify the original owner of lost property.

    d. All of the above.

21. The Louisiana Civil Code provides that "one who has possessed a movable object for more than 10 years acquires ownership by prescription." That statutory provision differs from the New Jersey's Supreme Court's decision in *O'Keeffe v. Snyder* insofar as the Louisiana statute (but not *O'Keeffe v. Snyder*):

    a. Allows possession to develop into ownership.

    b. Only applies if the possessor purchased the object.

    c. Does not adopt a discovery rule.

    d. Does not require registry in a database of lost objects.

22. Laura's favorite sheep wandered off of her property and onto the land owned by her neighbors, the Broens. Two days later, Elsa saw the sheep there and took it to her home. Who owns the sheep now?

ANSWER:

23. A voter mailed in an absentee ballot with no return address during New Campbell's most recent gubernatorial election. The vote did not count because there was no identification on it. But the envelope caught the interest of the election workers because it was mailed with a rare stamp worth $100,000. Once the story was reported in the local (and soon the national) news, the voter identified herself as Martha Hiddelheimer, and authorities were able to confirm that she mailed the ballot with the $100,000 stamp. Martha explained that she had no idea that the stamp was so valuable, and she asked for it back. She won't get it back, though, because the stamp was:

    a.   Abandoned.

    b.   Lost.

    c.   Mislaid.

    d.   Treasure trove.

24.   In November 1991, I proposed to my fianceé Lisa. She read a letter that I had written, then I asked her to marry me, at which point she began sobbing and repeating "I don't know what to say." I told her to say "yes," and she said "yes." Then I put a sapphire and diamond ring on her finger. We were married in May 1992. When did (or does) the ring become unconditionally Lisa's?

ANSWER:

25.   Wenceslao was detained by the Immigration and Naturalization Service (INS) in San Antonio. His friend Jose took $15,000 in cash from Jose's trust account to put up the cash bond for Wenceslao's release. When Amy and Jose arrived at the INS office, Jose asked Amy to go inside to post the cash bond because he was concerned that the INS would also detain him. Amy went in with the money, but the INS did not accept cash. So Amy and Jose went to a bank, Amy gave the cash back to Jose, and he secured a cashier's check payable to the INS with his name as the remitter. Jose then gave the check to Amy, who returned to the INS, posted the bond using the cashier's check, and obtained a receipt for it in her name. The cash bond was released after Wenceslao's INS case was resolved, so Jose told Amy that he wanted his money back. Amy's claim that she can keep the money because it was a gift from Jose will fail because there is insufficient evidence of:

    a.   Intent to make a gift.

    b.   Delivery of the gift.

    c.   Acceptance of the gift.

    d.   All of the above.

26.   One day while Wally was swimming in the Chariton River, he discovered that what he thought was a log protruding from the bank and partly inundated by the water was actually an old canoe. They showed it to Mr. Biegel, who, the following day, with his sons, excavated and removed it. No one knows how long the canoe had been in this spot. Wally learned that "the fertile valley of the Chariton River" had once been "the ancient hunting grounds of the mighty Osages." According to one expert, "how many years, or hundreds of years, it has taken the flood waters of the Chariton to deposit from 15 to 25 feet of silt over it, could only be estimated by learned geologists." In any event, Wally unearthed the canoe and plans to display it at the Missouri Museum of Native Americans. But Ellie Mae claims that the canoe actually belongs to her because she owns the land where the canoe was found. Who owns the canoe?

   a.   Wally, because the canoe was lost.

   b.   Wally, because the canoe is real property.

   c.   Ellie Mae, because the canoe is personal property.

   d.   Ellie Mae, because the canoe was embedded in the soil.

27.   Plaintiff and defendant had adjoining duplex apartments in a two-family house owned by the defendant. Each duplex had two floors and a basement. Plaintiff rented his apartment from the defendant starting in January 1952, and, with defendant's permission, immediately took exclusive possession of the basement belonging to that apartment. Plaintiff testified that in January or February 1953, he determined to paint his living room fireplace, which had been soiled by Christmas decorations; and he went down to the basement, where he recalled seeing some old paint cans. On a shelf about six feet high and two and one-half or three feet wide, plaintiff found a dusty green lunch box hidden behind the paint cans on the extreme rear of the shelf. The box contained $10,500 in American currency. He and his wife then went next door and told defendant of their discovery. Plaintiff's best argument for keeping the money is that:

   a.   The original owner lost the money.

   b.   The money was abandoned.

   c.   Plaintiff possesses the premises.

   d.   Plaintiff is a bona fide purchaser.

28.   Patricia inherited a sapphire ring from her grandmother. She gave the ring to Crockett & Sons, a local jeweler, to be cleaned. After cleaning the ring, Crockett & Sons placed it in a display case and sold the ring to Alexandra. Once the mistake was discovered, Patricia asked Alexandra for the ring back, but she refused to return it. Patricia's lawsuit against Alexandra will:

   a.   Succeed, because Crockett & Sons acted contrary to its bailment.

   b.   Succeed, because Alexandra was not a bona fide purchaser.

   c.   Fail, because Alexandra is a bona fide purchaser.

   d.   Fail, because Crockett & Sons held void title to the ring.

29.   Late one night, Paula Paparazzi tracked down a famous politician and an equally famous movie star as they engaged in a romantic encounter in a secluded part of a public beach. As they left, Paula noticed that something had fallen from the movie star's neck onto the sand. Paula waited until they were a safe distance away, ran to the spot where they had been, and picked up the locket that was sitting there. The locket contained the seal of the United States Senate, and it was inscribed, "For Lucretia, my lover, from your favorite Senator," and it was dated from the year before. The locket was tarnished, though, so Paula wanted to clean it before she publicized the relationship that she had discovered. So Paula

took the locket to the nearby StuffMart, which promised to polish any jewelry at any time, day or night. Paula dropped off the locket, left for an hour to get something to eat, and returned for the polished locket. But when she arrived at the counter in the StuffMart, there was a "closed until the morning" sign there. A few days later, Paula was horrified to learn that locket was being advertised for sale at StuffMart. Paula immediately drove to the store and demanded the locket back. But Lucretia and the Senator had learned of the locket by this time, and they each demanded it, too. Who owns the locket?

a. The Senator.

b. Lucretia.

c. Paula.

d. StuffMart.

30. Dr. Gomez is a medical researcher who developed a new stem cell line. One of his students was jealous of Gomez, so he destroyed all of Gomez's work. If Gomez sues the student for conversion, Gomez will likely:

a. Win, because the stem cell line is property protected by a conversion action.

b. Lose, because the stem cell line is not property for any purposes.

c. Lose, because a conversion action is not allowed in such circumstances.

d. Lose, both because the stem cell line is not property for any purposes and because a conversion action is not allowed in such circumstances.

31. At their high school graduation, Laura wanted to give her favorite old doll to her best friend Julia. Julia said thanks, but she insisted that she was not interested in taking such a valuable childhood treasure from Laura. Laura pleaded with Julia to think about it, so they sat the doll on a public bench as they entered a nearby restaurant for dinner. During dinner, Laura convinced Julia to keep the doll. Only then did they realize that they did not have it. They looked everywhere and asked everyone in the building, but no one remembered seeing the doll. Nor did anyone respond to the notices that they posted around the school and near the restaurant. Instead, one week later, a friend of Julia's saw that the doll had been offered for auction on eBay. Julia contacted Ellen, the seller, who said that she found the doll in the trash outside the building where Laura and Julia had left it. But Margaret had already won the auction on eBay, and she had already received the doll from Ellen. Who is the owner of the doll?

a. Laura.

b. Julia.

c. Ellen.

d. Margaret.

32. Andy stole a watch from Betsy, who found it along the beach where it had been dropped by Cara, who found it on a counter in the Dickens grocery store, where it was left by Esther, who inherited it from her grandmother. The police recovered the watch when they arrested Andy, but Esther has no idea what happened to the watch despite repeated efforts of the police, Cara, Betsy, and the Dickens grocery store to identify the original owner. Which of these parties has the best claim to own the watch?

    a. Andy.

    b. Betsy.

    c. Cara.

    d. The Dickens grocery store.

33. Aunt Sue gave her nieces Laura and Julia gifts of $2,000 every year for Christmas. In December 2004, she instructed her financial manager to transfer $1,000 worth of her shares in H.J. Heinz Company stock to each niece and to give each niece $1,000 in cash. The financial manager transferred the title to the stock, but he accidentally wrote each niece a $1,000 check from an old, closed checking account. Laura and Julia discovered the mistake when the bank refused to cash their checks. Alas, Aunt Sue had died the day before, and now her sole heir Ivy claims that she is the owner of the $4,000 that Aunt Sue meant to give to her nieces. Laura and Julia each have a property right to:

    a. The stock and the $1,000 from the checking account.

    b. The stock, but not the $1,000.

    c. The $1,000, but not the stock.

    d. Neither the stock nor the $1,000.

34. Norma inherited several pieces of her grandmother's furniture in 1975. At the time of her grandmother's death, Norma lived out of state and did not have a place to store her inherited property. Lewis and Virginia Martin, Norma's uncle and his wife, volunteered to store her inherited property in a cottage on their farm. Norma accepted their offer knowing that Virginia stored her antiques there and that their property would be commingled. The Martins never charged Norma for storing her property nor did they use her property. Norma visited the Martins over the years, and she checked on her property when she was there, most recently in 2005. She admitted the cottage was full of furniture and she could not see all of her property, but the items she did see were in satisfactory condition. Then Norma died in 2009, and her heirs discovered that much of her property has been damaged and destroyed during the past 30 years by water entering the cottage through an unknown leak in the roof. Norma's heirs' lawsuit against the Martins will:

    a. Succeed, because the Martins served as bailees for hire.

    b. Succeed, because the Martins are responsible for any damage that occurs on their property.

c. Fail, because the Martins accepted a gratuitous bailment.

d. Fail, because the damage was caused by water.

35. Ann bought a new car. She allowed her son James, a recent college graduate, to drive the car whenever he needed it even though the car remained titled in only Ann's name. Three months later, James gave the car to William in order to satisfy a $25,000 gambling debt. William then forged a new title and sold the car to Helmkamp Motors, a local car dealer, for $20,000. Who owns the car now?

a. Ann.

b. James.

c. William.

d. Helmkamp Motors.

36. The product pictured here does not violate the Louis Vuitton trademark because:

   a. There is a First Amendment free speech right to engage in parody.

   b. It is not likely that consumers will believe that Louis Vuitton is the source of the product.

   c. It uses different colors than the Louis Vuitton trademark.

   d. The Louis Vuitton trademark originated in France.

37. In *Bilida v. McLeod*, where local authorities seized and killed a raccoon that the Bilida family had kept as a pet for 12 years, the Bilidas would have been able to keep their pet raccoon if:

   a. The raccoon did not have rabies.

   b. They had a permit for the raccoon.

   c. Rhode Island had enacted a statute treating pets as "companion animals."

   d. They had captured the raccoon from the wild.

38. Your right knee is your property in sense that it is legal to:

   a. Sell it.

   b. Destroy it.

   c. Give it to someone else.

   d. Use it.

39. Paul Jackson spent two years making "The Tiger Spot," a mosaic consisting of glass tiles that the University of Missouri installed in a prominent place on campus. Jackson alleges that the university damaged The Tiger Spot by failing to use proper materials and engineering, not protecting the mosaic from rain, and allowing excessive traffic on the mosaic. If that is true, then the university could be liable for violating which law?

ANSWER:

40. Albert Einstein died in New Jersey in 1955 with a will that gave "all of my manuscripts, copyrights, publication rights, royalties and royalty agreements, and all other literary property and rights, of any and every kind or nature whatsoever to my secretary Helena Dukas for life, and then to Hebrew University." Dukas died in 1978. In 2009, General Motors placed an advertisement featuring Einstein's photo in *People* magazine's Sexiest Man Alive edition. Hebrew University's claim that General Motors and *People* violated Einstein's right of publicity is most likely to fail if:

   a. New Jersey holds that the right of publicity is not descendible.

   b. Dukas conveyed all of the rights that she received from Einstein to General Motors before she died.

   c. Federal copyright law deems the publication of Einstein's photo a fair use.

   d. New Jersey did not recognize a right of publicity until 1966.

41. Which of the following cannot be copyrighted?

   a. A Thomas & Friends toy train.

   b. A photograph of a Thomas & Friends toy train.

   c. An article about a Thomas & Friends toy train.

   d. A song about a Thomas & Friends toy train.

42. Missy Chase Lapine published a cookbook entitled "The Sneaky Chef: Simple Strategies for Hiding Healthy Foods in Kids' Favorite Meals." Four months later, Jerry Seinfeld (yes, really) published a cookbook entitled "Deceptively Delicious: Simple Secrets to Get Your Kids Eating Good Food." Why will Lapine's trademark suit against Seinfeld fail?

ANSWER:

43. Sam Keller was a starting quarterback for the Arizona State University and University of Nebraska football teams. In its "NCAA Football" video games, EA depicts a virtual player who wears the same jersey number, is the same height and weight, plays the same way, and hails from the same state as Keller. EA's best response to Keller's right of publicity claim is that:

a. The depiction of the virtual player qualifies as fair use.

b. Few people know who Keller is.

c. The virtual player in "NCAA Football" wears different shoes than Keller.

d. The first amendment protects EA's use of a virtual player resembling Keller.

44. In 2008, Susan Elizabeth wrote "The History of Wisco '99,'" which tells the tale of an obscure gasoline company that went out of business in 1978. Shockingly, the book became a best-seller. Elisha Coffman has developed a website that seeks to help her get rich by taking advantage of Wisco "99"'s newfound fame. Which aspect of the website is most likely to violate a provision of intellectual property law?

a. The use of the Wisco "99" symbol on the home page.

b. A description of Wisco "99"'s patented formula for gasoline.

c. A reproduction of the table of contents from "The History of Wisco '99.'"

d. A photo of Susan Elizabeth.

45. Most parodies of trademarks do not violate the Lanham Act because:

a. The First Amendment protects parodies as free speech.

b. The Lanham Act does not protect against the use of similar trademarks.

c. Consumers are not likely to be confused about the source of the parody.

d. Consumers are likely to gain a better impression of the trademark.

46. Which of the following animals is most likely to be lawfully possessed by the Robinson family?

a. Goldy, a golden eagle that the family has cared for as a pet since the bird was abandoned in its nest on the family's land.

b. Bambi, a deer that the family rescued from a hunter whose shot had wounded it and who was about to kill the deer.

c. Simba, a labrador retriever who lives with the family in their home in Rhode Island, where a state statute refers to pets as companions instead of as being owned.

d. Al, a donkey that lives on the family's property in a part of the county that is zoned to forbid landowners from keeping any animals.

47. During the 19th century, surgery was always a highly dangerous medical procedure because patients could die of shock from the trauma of the operation, wholly unrelated to the ailment which occasioned the operation. Then Dr. Morton began to use ether vapor to anesthetize patients during surgical operations. Morton thus applied for, and received, a patent. Undeterred, the New York Eye Infirmary started to use ether vapor as an anaesthetic during its surgical procedures. Morton's suit for infringement of a patent will:

a. Succeed, because the infirmary failed to challenge the patent when it was issued.

b. Succeed, if no one had thought about using ether as an anaesthetic before he did.

c. Fail, if the effect of ether when inhaled was obvious.

d. Fail, because the common law does not grant inventors the exclusive right to their inventions.

48. Copyright's fair use doctrine operates as an exception to which property right?

ANSWER:

49. Which property right is *least* likely to apply to your own body?

a. The right to alienate.

b. The right to manage.

c. The right to exclude.

d. The right to use.

50. Why does a parody of a trademark not necessarily violate that trademark?

ANSWER:

51. On August 7, 1981, Van Wert County conveyed a lot next to the county courthouse "to the Pittsburgh, Ft. Wayne and Chicago Railway Co., so long as said strip may be required or used for passenger station purposes only; but in the event that said lot shall be finally vacated and abandoned for passenger station purposes, then, and in that event the same shall revert to Van Wert County." What interest did the railway company acquire?

ANSWER:

52. Which of the following conveyances includes a valid springing executory interest?

   a. O conveys "to A if A becomes a millionaire."

   b. O conveys "to B, but if B becomes a doctor, then to X."

   c. O conveys "to C for life, then to X if X outlives C, but if C outlives X, then to Y."

   d. O conveys "to D when the Chicago Cubs win the World Series."

53. Dr. Hillery W. Key died in 1912 with a will providing that "I desire and will that my real estate shall be enjoyed by my children during their lives as tenants in common; then by my grandchildren during their lives and then by my great-grandchildren who reach the age of 21." The devise to the great-grandchildren:

   a. Is not subject to the rule against perpetuities.

   b. Satisfies the rule against perpetuities using Dr. Key's children as the measuring life.

   c. Satisfies the rule against perpetuities using Dr. Key's grandchildren as the measuring life.

   d. Violates the rule against perpetuities.

54. The owner of a life estate may not:

   a. Convey her interest to someone else.

   b. Devise the property to her children in a will.

   c. Erect any permanent structures.

   d. All of the above.

55. On April 26, 2005, Kim conveyed her lakefront property "to Ron, but if Ron ever files for bankruptcy, then to Eric." Ron is 25 years old, and he has never filed for bankruptcy. What interest does Eric own in the property?

ANSWER:

56. Albert Luth executed a last will and testament in 1957 that devised the land he had owned "to Dr. Kurt DeJong so long as the property is used to provide medical care, and then to Benton County." What interest does Benton County now own in the property?

ANSWER:

57. Julia sold her favorite pasture land "to Lisa for life, then to the first grandson of Lisa to marry Laura." Which of the following statements is most likely to be correct?

    a. Lisa owns a life estate.

    b. Lisa's grandson Andrew owns a contingent remainder.

    c. Lisa owns the property in fee simple.

    d. Lisa's grandson Benjamin owns an executory interest.

58. Which of the following conveyances contains a fee simple subject to a condition subsequent?

    a. O conveys to B for life, then to C.

    b. O conveys to B so long as the property is used for a school, then to C.

    c. O conveys to B provided that the property is used for a hospital.

    d. O conveys to B if B turns 21 before O dies.

59. Which of the following conveyances gives Dave a valid executory interest?

    a. O conveys to A for life, then to Dave.

    b. O conveys to A for life, then to Susan, but if Susan writes a best-selling novel, then to Dave.

    c. O conveys to A for life, then to Susan if any of her preschool students write a novel that makes the "Book of the Century" list announced in 2100, then to Dave.

    d. O conveys to Dave so long as Susan teaches preschool.

60. Thomas R. Jenkins died on June 30, 2013. The provisions of his will read as follows: "To my wife, I give and bequeath all my property both personal and real, as long as she remains

my widow, should she marry again, then in this event, my property is to be divided equally between my children and it is my wish that they share and share alike." What interest do Thomas's children hold in the property?

ANSWER:

61. In 1964, Jane Buntin conveyed to the Ladies' Hermitage Association (LHA) the Tulip Grove house originally built by President Andrew Jackson's nephew in the 19th century. The conveyance stated that LHA "shall own Tulip Grove provided that LHA pays to Buntin at least $600 annually in gate receipts received from tourists visiting Tulip Grove." What property interest do Buntin's heirs have in Tulip Grove?

ANSWER:

62. Which of the following conveyances violates the Rule against Perpetuities?

   a. In 2009, O conveyed Blueacre "to A so long as the property contains a hot tub."

   b. In 2009, O devised Greenacre "to A for life, then to B, but if any dandelions are seen on the property, then to C."

   c. In 2000, O conveyed Orangacre "to A for life, then to B for life, then to C, but if C moves to North Carolina, then to D."

   d. In 2000, O conveyed Purpleacre "to A for 10 years, then to B for 10 years, then to A's children, but if A doesn't have a daughter, then to D."

63. In 2011, Leanna wrote a will stating that "I now give, devise and bequeath Wynbrooke Plantation to Sara, but if Sara ever gets married, then in such case I do devise all of my property to Anna." In 2012, Sara sold all of her property — real and personal — to Jeff for $480,000, which Sara used to pay for college. Leanna died in July 2013. Two weeks later, Sara graduated from college; she remains unmarried. Who owns the present possessory interest in Wynbrooke Planatation?

   a. Leanna's heirs.

   b. Sara.

   c. Anna.

   d. Jeff.

64. Ruby owned a farm that has been in her family for four generations, and she wanted to ensure that it would remain in the family. So on December 6, 2005, Ruby quitclaimed a life estate interest in her 120-acre farm to herself, and a remainder to her son Kurt. One day later, Kurt died in a car accident. Kurt did not have a will, and his two young sons who live with his ex-wife are his heirs. Who owns what interest in the farm?

    a.   Ruby owns the farm in fee simple; Kurt's sons have no interest.

    b.   Ruby owns a life estate; Kurt's sons have a vested remainder.

    c.   Ruby owns a life estate; Kurt's sons have a contingent remainder.

    d.   Ruby has no interest; Kurt's sons own the farm in fee simple.

65.   In 1939, Clatsop County, Oregon conveyed a lot "to the City of Seaside, provided that the property shall be used by the City for municipal purposes and for no other purpose, and in the event that the same shall not be used or continue to be so used, then said real property and the whole thereof shall revert to Clatsop County, without any Act of or by Clatsop County." The city built and operated a municipal pumping station on the lot until 1990. In 1993, the city sold the lot to Jessie for $300,000, and he lived there and ran a candy store there until he died intestate last month. The county has never objected to Jessie's use of the lot. Who owns the lot?

    a.   Clatsop County.

    b.   The City of Seaside.

    c.   Jessie's heirs.

    d.   The State of Oregon.

66.   Lisa owns a contingent remainder in which of the following conveyances:

    a.   Olivia conveys "to Julia so long as she uses the property to board horses, and then to Lisa."

    b.   Olivia conveys "to Julia for life, and then to Lisa and her heirs."

    c.   Olivia conveys "to Julia for life, then to Laura for life, then to Lisa if she is still living, and if Lisa is not living then to John."

    d.   Olivia conveys "to Julia for life, and one year after Julia's death, then to Lisa."

67.   In 2002, Linda Klein Jackson died with a will leaving her lake home "to Andrew for life, then to such of the grandchildren of Andrew who reach the age of 21." At the time of Linda's death, Andrew was 43 years old, and he had two daughters Katy and Christina. Upon Linda's death, Andrew owned which interest in the lake home?

ANSWER:

68.   Juan Martinez wants to dispose of most of his property holdings before he retires from his job as a real estate agent. Toward that end, Juan sold 20 acres of undeveloped land "to Angela so long as it is not developed." Two weeks later, Bob sold his remaining interest in the undeveloped land "to Bob's widow and her heirs." At the time of the conveyance, Angela is 56 years old, Bob is 72 years old, and Bob's wife Elizabeth is 70 years old. Angela owns:

a. A fee simple absolute.

b. A fee simple determinable.

c. A fee simple subject to condition subsequent.

d. No interest in the property.

69. The Mountain Realty Company conveyed 10 acres of land "to Elaine for life." Two years later, Elaine drafted a will devising all of her property to her son Randy. Then Randy sold his interest in the land "to Sara so long as she does not allow a SUV to enter the property." Next Elaine sold the land "to the county for use as a park." Finally, Elaine died. Who owns the possessory interest in the 10 acres of land?

a. Mountain Realty Company.

b. Randy.

c. Sara.

d. The county.

70. After Lisa built a church building on land that she owned, she told the Providence Church that they could use the building and the land for church purposes. The Providence Church held worship services there until Lisa died 45 years later, devising her entire estate to Jenny. Lisa's son Andrew, however, believed that he was entitled to the land as Lisa's sole heir, and Andrew repeatedly wrote to the Providence Church demanding that they stop using the property. The Providence Church ignored the letters and continued holding its worship services there for another 25 years. Who is the rightful owner of the land?

a. The Providence Church.

b. Andrew.

c. Jenny.

d. Andrew and Jenny as tenants in common.

TOPIC 5:	15 QUESTIONS
CONCURRENT OWNERS	

71. Which of the following partition actions is *least* likely to be granted?

    a. A joint tenant's application for a partition in kind.

    b. A tenant in common who has a 5/8th interest in the property's application for a partition by sale.

    c. A tenant in common who has a 1/8th interest in the property's application for a partition in kind.

    d. The owner of a contingent remainder's application for a partition by sale.

72. Herman and Jerry acquired 160 acres of land in 1924 as tenants in common. Herman died in 1931, leaving all of his property to his widow, Margaret, and his three daughters from a previous marriage, Julia, May, and Jennie. Twenty years later, in 1951, Margaret, Julia, May, and Jennie executed a deed conveying their interest in the property to May's husband, Earl. Earl promptly deeded his newly-acquired interest in the property back to Margaret, Julia, May, and Jennie, specifically providing "not in tenancy in common but in joint tenancy." All of the parties died without a will over the next 50 years: first Jennie, then May, then Jerry, then Earl, then Margaret, then Julia. Who owns the property now?

ANSWER:

73. A tenancy by the entirety provides that:

    a. The husband and wife each own half of the property.

    b. The husband and wife are co-tenants in whatever proportion they desire.

    c. The wife and husband promise to divide their property equally if they divorce.

    d. The wife and husband own the property as a single entity.

74. Which of the following factors is most likely to be considered by a court in dividing property upon a divorce in a community property state?

    a. Fidelity during the marriage.

    b. Legal title to each asset.

    c. The division of household responsibilities during the marriage.

    d. The earning capacity of each spouse.

75. Rosebud E. Keys died on February 24, 2007, with a will providing that all of his property "shall go to Walter Rebeck and the Central Avenue United Methodist Church of Kansas City as joint tenants." Rebeck died in 2008. Then the church dissolved in 2009 and transferred its assets to the United Methodist Church, the national denomination of which the church had been a part. Who owns the property that Keys had owned when he died?

ANSWER:

76. Community property states differ from other states insofar as community property states:

    a. Do not allow either spouse to own any property separately.

    b. Limit the ability of each spouse to engage in non-wasteful use of the married couple's assets.

    c. Require an equal division of property if the spouses divorce.

    d. All of the above.

77. Claire, Kevin, and Ben own their home as joint tenants. In 2007, Ben sold his interest in the home to Jackson. In 2008, Kevin died with a will leaving all of his property to his daughters Stella and Millie. In 2009, Claire conveyed her interest in the home to Becky. Who owns what interest in the home?

ANSWER:

78. Which of the following is most likely to be a factor in determining the division of property upon divorce in a community property state?

    a. The length of the marriage.

    b. The fault of the party who caused the divorce.

    c. Who owns the title to the property.

    d. All of the above.

79. On August 1, 2000, the Federal Land Bank conveyed a parcel of land to "Nathan and Alice as joint tenants, and not as tenants in common, to them and their assigns and to the survivor, and the heirs and assigns of the survivor forever." Nathan and Alice were married at the time, but they got divorced in June 2008. Nathan then conveyed his interest in the property to Frank and Roxa "as joint tenants and not as tenants in common, to them and their heirs and assigns, and to the survivor of them, and to the heirs and assigns of such survivor forever." And then Nathan died without a will. Who owns what interest in the property?

ANSWER:

80.   In 1975, Trudy conveyed nine acres of land "to Thomas, for and during his natural life and at his death to his heirs." In 2002, Thomas conveyed his interest in the land to "my wife Almedia and I, by a tenancy by the entirety." Thomas died in 2002 leaving only two heirs: his wife Almedia and his son Steve. Who owns what interest in the land?

ANSWER:

81.   In *United States v. Craft*, the U.S. Supreme Court's decision relied upon:

   a.   Michigan state law's definition of property.

   b.   The bundle of sticks metaphor.

   c.   The fact that many jurisdictions have abolished the tenancy by the entirety.

   d.   The biblical teaching that a married man and woman are one flesh.

82.   In 1999, William Aldridge drafted a will devising his farm "to Lance and Paula as joint tenants." In December 2001, Lance died. Two weeks later, William died. Who owns the farm?

   a.   Paula.

   b.   Lance's heirs and Paula as tenants in common.

   c.   Lance's heirs and Paula as joint tenants.

   d.   William's heirs.

83.   Jack and Jill were married in New Campbell, and they are now getting divorced there. Before they were married, Jill accumulated nearly $80,000 in student loans which they paid together while they were married. They also bought a house as joint tenants while they were married, and they acquired a credit card account which they both used. Now that they are separated, Jill continues to live in the house. Which of the following liabilities is Jill alone most likely to have to pay?

   a.   The student loan payments.

   b.   The debt on the credit card.

   c.   The mortgage on the house.

   d.   Rent for continuing to live in the house.

84.   In 1990, Anita and Greg were married in Texas, where they lived for nine years until they couple separated in the summer of 2001. Greg drove a pickup truck that the couple bought

in 2000, while Anita drove an old sports car. Shortly after they separated, and Greg had moved out of their house, Anita went to his new home. Greg was sitting in his pickup truck in the driveway, and Anita parked behind him, blocking him in. Anita tried to "talk" to Greg, but he remained in his locked vehicle. When Greg would not roll his window down, Anita returned to her car and grabbed her keys. She then used the keys to severely scratch the paint on the passenger side and tailgate of Greg's truck. Subsequently, Greg sued Anita for damaging his property. Greg's lawsuit will:

a. Succeed because Anita had no property interest in the pickup truck.

b. Succeed because Anita's actions constituted waste.

c. Fail if Anita held the title to the truck.

d. Fail because Anita had the right to damage their truck.

85. David and Sarah were married in 1983, and soon thereafter they acquired 30 acres of land as tenants in common. The couple divorced in 1990. Upon their divorce, David conveyed his interest in the land "to Sarah so long as she lives within fifty miles of Salt Lake City." In 1998, Sarah sold the land to Hall Realty, but she continued to reside near Salt Lake City. In 2003, however, Sarah moved to North Carolina. Who owns the 30 acres of land?

ANSWER:

TOPIC 6: LANDLORDS, TENANTS, AND HOUSING

10 QUESTIONS

86. Janice has just moved to College Town, where she is in her first year of graduate school. She would like to live in a house owned by CT Realty because of a friend's recommendation and because of its proximity to her classes. In fact, she was so desperate to live in the house that she agreed to start paying $900 per month rent while she worked on a formal lease with CT Realty. After a few weeks, though, Janice and CT Realty were unable to agree upon a formal lease. How long can Janice can stay in the house?

ANSWER:

87. In January 1995, Lance Landlord leased his country estate to Thelma Tenant for 10 years at a monthly rent of $10,000. Thelma immediately moved into the estate. Then in August 2000, while Thelma was out of the country on a weekend trip, Francis Freeloader moved into the estate and installed her bodyguards to prevent anyone — including Thelma — from entering the property. It took Thelma four months to get the local government to evict Francis so that Thelma could move back into the estate in December 2000. Thelma refused to pay Lance any rent for the four months that Francis possessed the house. Which resulting lawsuit is most likely to be successful?

    a. Lance's suit against Thelma for the $40,000 unpaid rent.

    b. Lance's suit against Francis for the $40,000 unpaid rent.

    c. Thelma's suit against Lance for breach of an implied covenant if the American rule applies.

    d. Thelma's suit against Lance for breach of an implied covenant if the English rule applies.

88. Which rent control ordinance is most likely to be held unconstitutional?

    a. An ordinance that omits a declaration that it is responding to a wartime emergency.

    b. An ordinance that determines the permissible rent that a landlord may charge by calculating the sum of the landlord's operating expenses and debt service and then ensuring that the landlord receives gross rents greater than that amount.

    c. An ordinance that determines the permissible rent that a landlord may charge by authorizing the landlord to raise rents at one-half the annual rate of inflation.

    d.   An ordinance that allows the children of a tenant to remain in the apartment at the same rent once the tenant dies.

89.   Tori and Janice Paul rented a home to Reginald Carter. The Pauls will not be liable for breaching an implied warranty of habitability if:

    a.   Carter had signed a written waiver of the warranty when he agreed to lease the apartment.

    b.   The problems that Carter complained about did not exist at the time that his lease commenced.

    c.   They had tried but failed to fix the problems that Carter complained about.

    d.   Carter had rented a retail store from them.

90.   The Utah Mobile Home Park Residency Act prohibits the owner of a mobile home park from terminating a resident's lease without cause. The statute thus modifies which common law tenancy?

    a.   Term of years.

    b.   Periodic tenancy.

    c.   Both term of years and periodic tenancy.

    d.   Neither term of years nor periodic tenancy.

91.   On March 20, 1998, Jackson signed a lease to rent Dave's vacation home in southern Virginia for a two-year period from June 1, 1998, to May 31, 2000. Eager to enjoy the home, Jackson drove across the country with his family to begin their vacation. But when they arrived on June 4, 1998, the house was occupied by four different individuals. According to the American rule, Dave has breached an implied covenant with respect to each of the following individuals found at the house *except*:

    a.   Dave himself, who decided he really liked the house.

    b.   Dave's son Kyle, who received his dad's permission to use the house for a fishing trip.

    c.   Bob Clauss, who produces a deed indicating that he owns the house, and Dave does not own the house.

    d.   John Crosby, who grew up in the neighborhood and always wanted to spend some time in the house.

92.   Which tenant is most likely to be able to leave her premises without having to pay further rent or otherwise honor the terms of the lease?

    a.   Despite Linus Landlord's repeated repair attempts, the water in Tanya Tenant's apartment has not worked since she moved in six weeks ago.

b. The air conditioning in Terri Tenant's apartment breaks down on an afternoon when it is 104 degrees outside, and Lou Landlord tells her that he will not be able to fix it until the next day.

c. Twyla Tenant suspects that the two men who live in the apartment unit next to her are dealing drugs.

d. The lock on the front door of Tori Tenant's store has not worked since she rented the premises 13 months ago, but Larry Landlord tells her that she should fix it herself.

93. Roberto owns two acres of land on the outskirts of Chicago that he leased to Julia for 10 years beginning on April 21, 1998. It is now December 15, 1999. Which of the following agreements is most likely to be judged a sublease?

a. Julia rents the two acres to Franklin for the period from December 15, 1999, to April 21, 2008.

b. Julia rents one acre to Franklin for the period from December 15, 1999, to April 21, 2008.

c. Julia rents two acres to Franklin for the period from December 15, 1999, to April 21, 2006.

d. Julia one acre to Franklin for the period from December 15, 1999, to April 21, 2008.

94. Susan does not want to ever speak to her landlord Isaac again. She wants to know whether she will be able to move out of her apartment without informing Isaac that she is leaving or without Isaac informing her that he wants to end the lease, no matter how long she has to wait. She will be able to do so if she has which interest in the land?

ANSWER:

95. Rachel entered into a lease with Apartments, Inc., to rent an apartment. The lease signed by the parties provides that it may be terminated by either party "upon zero days notice." The most likely characterization of the lease is that it creates what interest in the land?

ANSWER:

TOPIC 7:
TITLE, OWNERSHIP, AND POSSESSION

10 QUESTIONS

96. Compliance with a recording system:

    a. Enables others to determine whether there are any easements burdening the property.

    b. Guarantees that the party recording their claim will prevail against any other claimants.

    c. Provides public notice about any latent defects in the property.

    d. Precludes any future adverse possession claims.

97. The Carlsons own a lot near Horseshoe Lake. Specifically, their lot is to the west of Leocadia Park, which is a privately-owned part that borders the lake to the east. They want to build a dock that allows them to anchor their sailboat that they use on the lake. They will be able to build the dock if:

    a. Their dock does not interfere with other users of the lake.

    b. They do not cross the park to get from their property to the lake.

    c. They receive the permission of the park's owners.

    d. New Campbell is a prior appropriation state.

98. In 2009, Hui Son Lye began voicing her concern that the Sacred Heart Catholic Church was not giving its Mass in Korean, despite her claim that the Archbishop had so instructed. Lye then engaged in threatening and harassing actions against parish personnel, and generally disrupted church services. The church then ordered Lye not to enter its property. If Lye returns to the church's property anyway, she will be:

    a. A trespasser.

    b. Acting within her rights under RLUIPA.

    c. Acting within her right to cultural property.

    d. Allowed to stay or not depending on the city's zoning law.

99. In June 2007, Peacock Point agreed to sell a six-lot waterfront subdivision in Destin, Florida, to Thomas J. Duggan for $3.2 million. In January 2008, Duggan sued Peacock Point, seeking to rescind the contract because the lots were not immediately ready for

residential construction. Duggan's lawsuit will:

a. Succeed, because Peacock Point had a duty to prepare the property for residential construction.

b. Succeed, because Duggan would not have paid $3.2 million if he knew the lots were not ready for residential construction.

c. Fail, because $3.2 million was a reasonable price for the property.

d. Fail, if the deed provided that Duggan purchased the property "as is."

100. The City of Blue River has long been a leading port for international trade. Recently, though, shipping vessels have been avoiding the city's port because the namesake Blue River has become filled with silt that blocks large ships from entering it. To remedy that problem, the city wants to dredge an area next to the Audubon wildlife sanctuary, but the sanctuary worries that the dredging will harm the wildlife there. The sanctuary's best argument against the dredging is:

a. The city failed to get the permit required by the federal Clean Water Act.

b. A riparian owner such as the sanctuary has the right to block any action that interferes with its use of the water.

c. The city is engaged in a trespass because the sanctuary owns the right to use the river.

d. An action that harms wildlife is a private nuisance.

101. Frederica bought an old house from Julia in a fashionable downtown neighborhood. Six months later, while Frederica was building an addition onto the back of her house, she noticed an orange substance oozing into her basement. She soon learned that the property had been used by the Acme Chemical Company 50 years ago, and that the substance was a toxic waste buried there by Acme and never seen since then — until now. Which of the following statements is true?

a. Frederica will have to pay to clean up the wastes.

b. Julia will have to pay to clean up the wastes.

c. Frederica can void her purchase of the house.

d. Julia is liable to Frederica for misrepresentation.

102. Jim hit a golf ball that sailed over Tim's house and then landed back on the golf course. Tim's trespass claim against Jim will:

a. Succeed, because Jim's ball crossed over Tim's property.

b. Succeed, provided that Tim had warned Jim not to hit the ball over the house.

c. Fail, provided that Jim was not aiming in that direction.

    d.   Fail, because no one was hurt.

103. Norma Fuqua owns land that is burdened by an easement held by the Oncor Electric Delivery Company. The easement states that it is "for an electric transmission and distribution line and all necessary or desirable appurtenances over, across and upon Fuqua's land." It further gives Oncor "the right to trim or cut down trees or shrubbery to the extent, in the sole judgment of the Company, necessary to prevent possible interference with the operation of said line or to remove possible hazard thereto." There is an airstrip on Fuqua's property outside the easement, and Fuqua is an experienced pilot who sometimes flies his small planes under Oncor's high voltage power line when landing on his airstrip. In Oncor's lawsuit to prevent Fuqua from flying across the easement, Oncor will likely:

    a.   Win, because Oncor has the exclusive right to use the property subjected to the easement.

    b.   Win, if the flights constitute a hazard to Oncor's electric transmission lines.

    c.   Lose, because the ad coelom doctrine does not apply to airspace.

    d.   Lose, if the airstrip was on Fuqua's property before Oncor constructed the transmission lines.

104. On December 30, 1986, Ridgway entered into a 20-year lease of Plot No. 52 from Castle Nugent Farms. Ridgway purchased a herd of dairy cows from Castle Nugent Farms and equipment to run a dairy farm. Ridgway alleges that the cattle he purchased for the dairy operation grazed over all of the properties that Castle Nugent Farms owned, not just Plot No. 52. On August 4, 2004, Golden Resorts purchased the land, including Plot No. 52, from Castle Nugent Farms. From August 2004 through May 2010, Golden Resorts alleges that it regularly inspected the property and never observed any livestock or other signs of adverse possession on the property. Ridgway, however, asserts that during this time period he had cattle and horses on the property, had erected fences, drilled for wells, engaged in bush cutting, pond building, firebreak plowing, road cutting, installation of pipelines, water troughs, generator houses and well pump houses, as well as creating hay rolls. Who will win Ridgway's adverse possession suit to claim ownership of Plot No. 52?

ANSWER:

105. The Osgoods and the Stantons own lots with homes adjacent to each other in the Township of Wyoming. Cody Street runs between the Osgoods's and the Stantons's lots. In December 2011, the Township of Wyoming vacated Cody Street. In June 2012, the Osgoods moved a shed and other property onto the vacated street and also erected a fence on the vacated street. The Stantons believed that the shed and fence encroached upon the portion of Cody Street that became their property when the township vacated the road. Therefore, in May 2013, the Stantons sued the Osgoods, alleging that the Stantons "have treated the entire vacated 25 feet of the vacated strip of Cody Street as their own, have exercised exclusive control over the vacated street and have denied the Osgoods the right to enjoy the use of any portion of the vacated street." Assuming that the facts alleged by the Stantons are true,

why will their adverse possession claim nonetheless fail?

ANSWER:

106. Caribbean House acquired a tract of land in 1961. In 1968, it sold the eastern part of the tract that borders the Hudson River to the Yacht Club. The 1968 conveyance stated that Caribbean House granted an easement across its remaining western part of the tract to the Yacht Club "as a means of ingress and egress to River Road from the Yacht Club's land." Over the ensuing 40 years, the easement was used by club members, their guests, boat mechanics and detailers, police and fire department personnel, boat haulers, waste haulers, and members of the Auxiliary Coast Guard, all without incident. In 2010, however, the Yacht Club permitted a neighboring restaurant to use the easement for customers to park their cars on the Yacht Club's property. Caribbean House objected to Yacht Club allowing cars from a nearby restaurant located on River Road to park on Yacht Club's property. Caribbean House then notified Yacht Club of its objection to the restaurant's use of the easement. May the Yacht Club allow the restaurant to use its easement?

   a. Yes, because the restaurant's customers are using the easement for ingress and egress to River Road.

   b. Yes, because Caribbean House never objected to any of the other uses of the easement.

   c. No, because Caribbean House has an inalienable right to exclude others from its land.

   d. No, because an easement may not be used for the benefit of property other than the dominant estate.

107. A town fire department purchased 3.25 acres of land to build a new truck room and social hall. The only catch is that the land is within a subdivision whose covenants prohibit the sale of alcoholic beverages. The fire department's challenge to the enforcement of the covenant by one of the other landowners within the subdivision will most likely:

   a. Succeed, because there are three new liquor stores just outside the subdivision.

   b. Succeed, because 68 of the 77 landowners within the subdivision approve of the fire department's plans.

   c. Succeed, because none of the landowners within the subdivision objected when the fire department bought the property.

   d. Fail, because the covenant is valid and enforceable.

108. Herman purchased a farm in 1968. In 1973, Herman sold the eastern portion of the property to the Larsons, while retaining the western portion for himself. Herman reserved an appurtenant easement in the deed conveying title to the eastern portion of the property

that provided "[n]on-exclusive easement for ingress and egress over and across a strip of land 20 feet in width." Herman continued to use the gravel road within the easement to access his property, primarily for hunting purposes, until he sold his remaining parcel to Colin in 1978. Colin operated a commercial fish hatchery on the property until 1990. At that time, he sold the property to its current occupants, Phillip and Shannon Hintz. The Hintzes continued the fish hatchery business for the next 11 years. Much like Colin, the Hintzes's business invitees regularly used the gravel road to conduct business on the property. In 2001, the Hintzes ended their fish hatchery business and began hosting temporary outdoor events, such as weddings, on their property. In 2007, the Hintzes obtained a conditional use permit (CUP) from the Grant County Board of Commissioners permitting them to host up to 28 outdoor events each year. The Hintzes had been previously limited to conducting four or fewer of these events per year by county ordinance. After obtaining the permit, they conducted 18 events in 2007, 19 in 2008, and 14 in 2009. An average of 30 to 60 vehicles used the gravel road to reach the Hintzes' property for each event. But the annual amount of commercial traffic utilizing this road has not substantially differed from their previous business. Meanwhile, the eastern parcel of the farm was sold by the Larsons and eventually came into the possession of the Wilsons, who object to all of the traffic crossing their land to attend weddings and other outdoor events at the Hintzes's. Can the Wilsons exclude people from crossing their land to attend events at the Hintzes's?

    a.   Yes, because the Hintzes are engaged in a different business than Herman had done.

    b.   Yes, because the traffic is substantially interfering with the use and enjoyment of their land.

    c.   No, because the Hintzes are acting within the scope of the easement.

    d.   No, but they can recover just compensation from the county for approving the Hintzes's outdoor events.

109. John has an express easement to cross Lisa's land to get to the nearest highway. According to the *Restatement*, which of the following actions may be undertaken unilaterally depending on the circumstances?

    a.   John can use the easement for a different purpose.

    b.   John can use a different part of Lisa's land to access the highway.

    c.   Lisa can terminate the easement.

    d.   Lisa can require John to use a different part of her land to access the highway.

110. The establishment of an easement by necessity depends most on how the property has been used by:

    a.   The current owner of the property allegedly subject to the easement.

    b.   The previous owner of the property allegedly subject to the easement.

    c.   The party seeking to use the easement.

    d. The owner of the dominant tenement.

111. Rick Sowers informed residents of the Forest Hills Subdivision that he planned to construct a wind turbine on his residential property. After this announcement, the residents of the subdivision filed a complaint claiming that the proposed wind turbine posed a potential nuisance because it would generate constant noise and obstruct the views of neighboring properties. At the preliminary injunction hearing, the district court heard testimony that the subdivision was a very quiet area, and that the turbine would obstruct the viewer's view and create noise and "shadow flicker," i.e., the rotating wind turbine blades would cast shadows upon stationary objects. Another resident, who was also a licensed realtor, testified that the proposed wind turbine would diminish property values in the neighborhood. A renewable energy specialist testified that the proposed wind turbine would likely generate the same level of noise as "the hum of a highway," and a contractor hired to construct the turbine testified that there was no way to mitigate the shadow flicker caused by the wind turbine. The lawsuit filed by the subdivision will most likely:

    a. Succeed, because the harms resulting from the wind turbine constitute a private nuisance.

    b. Succeed, because the shadow flicker constitutes a trespass.

    c. Fail, because the federal policy promoting renewable energy preempts any state law claims.

    d. Fail, provided that the local zoning law permits wind turbines.

112. The Freys and the Corbins purchased neighboring parcels of land in 1990. Both properties are encumbered with a 259.91 foot long easement to be used as a private road for ingress and egress running east on either side of the common property line. The width of the 50-foot-wide private road is split equally between the two properties. A gravel driveway (the front portion of the easement) continued for about 40 feet until it split into separate driveways leading to the Freys's and the Corbins's respective properties. After the split, a fence separated the two halves of the easement between the properties. Initially, the Corbins used the easement as a private drive for tractor trailers to pull onto their property, but they stopped doing that once they extended the fence to deter thieves. Also, in 1992, the Corbins planted trees alongside the easement in a way that prevented them from using their side of the easement. The Freys have used the area within the easement on their side of the fence for camping and recreation purposes. In May 2012, the Corbins took down a portion of the fence and an elm tree on the Freys's side of the fence. The Freys were both away from home at this time, and the Freys sued the Corbins when they discovered what had happened. What is the current legal status of the easement?

ANSWER:

113. Which of the following actions if prohibited by a conservation easement?

    a. The owner of the easement wants to convey her interest to someone else.

b. The owner of the property burdened by the easement wants to sell the land that she owns.

c. The purchaser of the land from the original owner who agreed to the easement wants to dam the stream that provides the habitat protected by the easement.

d. The neighboring landowner wants to hunt wildlife that wanders onto her land.

114. The requirement of vertical privity is relevant to determining whether:

a. An easement can be implied.

b. A covenant runs with the land.

c. An easement runs with the land.

d. A covenant can be implied.

115. In 1999, the Natural Heritage Foundation (NHF) purchased an easement on 500 acres of old growth forests owned by the Thompson family. According to the easement, it was "for the purpose of the conservation and preservation of unique and scenic areas, the environmental and ecological protection of the forests, wetlands and their accompanying watershed, and to prevent development in a manner inconsistent with those conservation purposes." In 2002, the Thompsons sold the land to Eighteen Enterprises, which plans to build a championship golf course on 75 acres of the property. NHF objects that a golf course is inconsistent with the easement because of the introduction of chemicals used to keep the fairways green. Eighteen Enterprises:

a. Cannot use the land without NHF's permission.

b. Can build and operate the golf course if it receives a permit from the governmental authorities responsible for regulating wetlands.

c. Can build and operate the golf course if it agrees not to use chemicals or otherwise interfere with the ecology and other environmental qualities of the land.

d. Is not bound by the agreement between the Thompson family and NHF.

116. Mobil operated a bulk fuel storage facility on land that was zoned for industrial uses. In 1997, Mobil conveyed the property to Pizza Property Partners with a covenant providing that "the property shall be used for commercial/light industrial purposes only." In 2000, Pizza Property Partners conveyed the land to the Voice of the Cornerstone Church with a deed stating that the conveyance was "subject to all existing covenants." The church has converted the property into a worship facility, including a baptismal pool from one of the tank farm's fuel storage tanks. Mobil, however, is suing the church to cease its operations. Mobil will probably:

a. Win, because the covenant touches and concerns the land.

b. Win, because the use of the property contrary to the covenant violates local zoning law.

c. Lose, because enforcement of the covenant would violate RLUIPA.

d. Lose, because horizontal privity is lacking.

117. The Lincoln Theater was built in Columbus, Ohio in 1922 and was added to the National Registry of Historic Places in 2000. The theater was slated for demolition until the Capital City Community Urban Redevelopment Corporation (CCCURC) bought the theater in 1991. In 2002, CCCURC sold the theater to the Columbus Urban Growth Corporation (CUG) for $1 with a covenant stating that "the buyer agrees to (a) provide Saturday movies for children for $1 or less, and (b) install a bronze plaque on the theater's façade that commemorates the theater's history." Then, in April 2010, CUG sold the theater to Sony Enterprises, which plans to raze the historic building, show only first-run movies for $10, and replace the plaque with its own marker emphasizing the role of Sony in shaping movie history. Which part of Sony's plans is lawful?

a. Razing the historic building, because federal law does not prohibit the destruction of buildings that are on the National Registry of Historic Places.

b. Showing only $10 movies, because the Saturday $1 children's movie requirement does not touch and concern the land.

c. Replacing the plaque, because the new marker complies with the covenant.

d. All of the above.

118. Betty Beaver agreed to sell land for a home site to Karen Brumlow. In reliance on Beaver's agreement to sell, Brumlow cashed in her IRA and 401-K retirement plans, at a substantial penalty, to pay for the home and improvements. But then Beaver reneged on the agreement after Brumlow left Beaver's employment and started working for a competitor. Brumlow's lawsuit to force Beaver to sell the home site to her will:

a. Succeed, because Beaver committed waste.

b. Succeed, because Brumlow satisfies the requirements for an easement by estoppel.

c. Fail, if the agreement was verbal.

d. Fail, if Brumlow has not begun the actual construction of the home.

119. Blue Harvest, Inc. (BHI) is engaged in the commercial production of blueberries in Ottawa County. BHI owns land that is adjacent to two county roads. Ottawa County maintains its county roads during the winter, when salt is used to prevent the formation of ice on the highways and roads. BHI claims that droplets of salt-laden water are thrown into the air by passing vehicles and are then blown by the wind onto BHI's property. It further contends that this salt spray damages its blueberry bushes, which results in a loss of blueberry production from those bushes. BHI may have a valid claim for a:

a. Nuisance.

b. Trespass.

c. Taking.

d. All of the above.

120. From 1947 to 1967, Lester owned two forty-acre parcels that he farmed as one tract. Lester used a dirt road across the eastern parcel to reach the public highway from the western parcel. In 1967, Lester deeded the east forty-acre parcel to his son George and the west forty-acre parcel to his daughter Lylia. Cahoy then purchased the west parcel from Lylia in November 2007, and Springer purchased the east parcel from George in May 2008. From 1967 until 2007, when Cahoy purchased his property, the two parcels were owned separately but were rented to one person and were operated as one unit. After the Springer-Cahoy purchases, the east parcel became an isolated tract in the sense that it had no direct access to a public highway. In the spring of 2008, Cahoy put up no trespassing signs attempting to restrict Springer from crossing his parcel. Springer, however, continued to cross Cahoy's parcel to access her property. Consequently, in 2009, Cahoy locked the gates that provided access to his parcel. Is Springer's lawsuit to cross Cahoy's land likely to succeed?

ANSWER:

121. Phyllis and Nancy live on neighboring properties in a small town. Nancy uses a wood-burning stove to heat her home so that she can reduce her electricity consumption and thus reduce global warming. Phyllis, however, complains that the smoke from Nancy's stove makes her ill, burns her throat, and sometimes prevents her from sleeping at night. Phyllis's claim that Nancy engages in a nuisance will most likely:

a. Succeed, because Phyllis has demonstrated an unreasonable interference with her use of her land.

b. Succeed, but only if wood-burning stoves are prohibited by the local zoning ordinance.

c. Fail, because nuisance law does not recognize the harms suffered by Phyllis.

d. Fail, because the Nancy's environmental goals outweigh Phyllis's harm.

122. Bill Fry is a captain with the Texas Army National Guard who is serving in Afghanistan. Before he went overseas, he built a swing set for his young children to enjoy while he was away. But the Spring Hills Homeowners' Association alleges that the swing set violates the covenants applicable to Fry's property. Fry's best argument against the enforcement of the covenant is that:

a. The covenant does not touch and concern the land.

b. The homeowners' association lacks the necessary privity with Fry.

c. The covenant does not appear on the deed to Fry's property, even though it appears in the deeds of half of his neighbors.

d.   The homeowners' association has failed to demonstrate that anyone is harmed by the swing set.

123. The McConnells live in a house next to the St. Andrews Golf Course (in Ocean Springs, Mississippi — not in Scotland). The golf course has an easement for utilities and for access to utilities along the 25 feet of the McConnells' property that abuts the golf course. In 2008, the golf course installed a concrete golf cart path and placed out-of-bounds markers on the part of the McConnells' land that is subject to the easement. The McConnells removed the out-of-bounds markers, and they removed them again after they were reinstalled by the golf course. Now the golf course claims that it has the right to keep both the golf cart path and the out-of-bounds markers. The golf course's claims will:

a.   Succeed for the both the golf cart path and the out-of-bounds markers, because the golf course has obtained a prescriptive easement.

b.   Succeed for the out-of-bounds markers because it has established a prescriptive easement, but fail for the golf cart path because they are beyond the scope of the easement.

c.   Succeed for the golf cart path because it has established a prescriptive easement, but fail for the out-of-bounds markers because they are beyond the scope of the easement.

d.   Fail for both the golf cart path and the out-of-bounds markers, because they are beyond the scope of the express easement and because there is no prescriptive easement.

124. The Cosina del Lago Restaurant overlooks a lake that diners can view from the second-floor dining room. Jack Johnson owned the land between the restaurant and the lake, and he wanted to build four large residential homes there. Johnson needed to build a road across the restaurant's property in order to provide access to his four planned homes, so he entered into an agreement in which the restaurant gave him an easement "across the restaurant's land" in exchange for a covenant that "none of the houses on Johnson's land would interfere with the restaurant's view of the lake." David Milne then bought one of the lots from Johnson and built a three-story house that blocked the restaurant's view of the lake. The restaurant's lawsuit against Milne to obtain equitable relief for violating the covenant will most likely:

a.   Succeed, because the covenant runs with the land.

b.   Succeed, because the agreement satisfies the requirements for a real covenant.

c.   Fail, because the covenant does not run with the land.

d.   Fail, because the covenant is ambiguous.

125. Susie Bardin is the current owner of a parcel of property that she purchased from Merrill Lynch Mortgage Lending, Inc. Other than a thin strip of land leading out to Market Street, most of the property sits back from the street, to the north of an existing railroad line, and has access to West Market Street only by means of a crossing over the Wheeling and Lake Erie Railway Company's tracks. For more than 100 years, the various owners of this parcel

have gained ingress to it and egress to the street by using the same railroad crossing. The railroad gave notice that it intended to close the crossing, and Bardin wonders whether she has the legal right to continue using the crossing over the railroad's tracks to access her landlocked property. Which fact will be most helpful to Bardin's claim that she has both an easement by necessity and an easement by implication to cross the railroad's tracks?

a. The thin strip of land leading to Market Street is too small for a road.

b. Merrill Lynch used to own all of the land that is now owned by the railroad and by Bardin.

c. Bardin has used the railroad's land to access her property for 20 years.

d. The Wheeling and Lake Erie Railway Company does not intend to formally abandon its rail line.

126. Leo McGrane lived on a farm in rural Iowa. On July 27, 1955, Leo obtained an easement to use the land now owned by Kevin Maloney "for all lawful purposes connected with the use and enjoyment of McGrane's property for farm land, but for no other purposes." Donald McGrane inherited the property from his father, and he now uses the easement for pasture, a hay field, row crops, cutting firewood, hunting, and ATV riding. Maloney's suit objecting to the use of the land for hunting and ATV riding will:

a. Succeed, because the easement specifies the only activities that are permissible.

b. Succeed, because the easement terminated upon Leo's death.

c. Fail, because hunting and ATV riding are the most valuable current use of the land.

d. Fail, because McGrane is permitted to unilaterally change the scope of the easement provided that it does not result in any additional harm to Maloney.

127. A conservation easement is a form of:

a. Negative easement.

b. Easement by necessity.

c. Prescriptive easement.

d. Easement by implication.

128. During the nineteenth century, Benjamin Colburn owned hundreds of acres of land. In 1846 he made the following conveyance: "I hereby convey the three acres of land that I own between the railroad and the pond to the Northern Railroad for the benefit of grading and repairing its tracks, provided that I retain the right to use the land for my own benefit." Colburn kept the rest of the land, and he used the land that he sold to the Northern Railroad to access his home just north of the three acres that he sold to the railroad. Much later, in 1999, the Northern Railroad discontinued its operations and formally abandoned the stretch of tracks in the area once owned by Colburn. Now Burton owns the land

containing Colburn's old home, and Philip owns the three acres that was sold to the Northern Railroad in 1846. Does Burton have the right to use Philip's land to access his home?

ANSWER:

129. The Sluyters and the Hales own adjoining tracts of land. In 1991, they exchanged reciprocal easements "to provide for the common use of the driveways on the two tracts of land." In 2005, the state highway department used its eminent domain power to obtain part of the Hales' property, which made it impossible for the Hales to continue using the driveway. Instead, the Hales began to build a fence along the property line in order to better preserve their privacy. The fence is:

   a. Permitted, because the easement ended when the Sluyters could not longer use it.

   b. Permitted, provided that the Hales have another way of reaching their property.

   c. Not permitted, because it violates the easement.

   d. Not permitted, provided that the initial easement agreement satisfies the touch-and-concern requirement.

130. In 1978, Townsend installed a septic tank on his land, and he installed a septic leach field that extended onto Parcel C, which was owned by Nickell. Two years later, Nickell prepared to farm Parcel C, but Townsend told Nickell not to drive over the land because it would destroy his leach field. Nickell farmed the land anyway. Over the years, Townsend offered to pay Nickell for Parcel C, but Nickell always refused. Finally, Townsend brought suit. What interest does Townsend have in Parcel C?

ANSWER:

131. In 2001, Josephine Driessen conveyed two lots to Roscoe and Clara Mae Robinson subject to the following restrictions: "This conveyance is made by the Grantor and accepted by the Grantees subject to the restriction that these lots shall not be used for construction of any type of amusement building thereon, nor shall any type of amusement facility be operated thereon. It is further understood and agreed that ROSCOE ROBINSON and CLARA MAE ROBINSON, their Heirs and Assigns, shall not in any way alter or destroy the sand dunes existing on the property." Driessen kept the lot next to the lots that she sold to the Robinsons. Now the Robinsons want to clear the sand dunes to build a small refreshment stand. Driessen objects that such a stand would violate the restrictions. At trial, Drissen testified that the restrictions were added because they made her remaining property more valuable because they insured that it would preserve her unobstructed view down the beach. Driessen's testimony is designed to satisfy:

   a. The intent requirement.

   b. The touch-and-concern requirement.

    c. Horizontal privity.

    d. Vertical privity.

132. In 1960, the Dewey Refining Company sold Scott an easement to cross the company's land so that Scott could drive to his new home. Scott used the road across from the company's land for a few years, then he moved away from his home because of its bad memories associated with his former wife. In 1972, the company built a communications tower that blocked the road that Scott had used across its land. Scott never complained, but after Scott died in 2008, his daughter Shelley wanted to live in the house that she inherited from her father. Why does Shelley not have a right to use the road?

ANSWER:

133. Lance Jones has suffered from alcoholism since he was in a car accident nearly 20 years ago. In August 1999, he purchased a unit in the Pacific Vistas condominiums near the beach in Carmel, California. As part of the purchase, he signed an agreement containing a covenant stating that "the owner shall keep the premises free of any pornographic materials." Shortly after Lance moved in, two children playing in an adjacent yard notified their parents that they had seen Lance viewing pornographic web sites while surfing the internet on his porch. The Pacific Vistas Homeowner's Association — of which his unit is a part — has fined Lance $1,000 for violating the covenant. Lance's argument against paying the fine will likely:

    a. Succeed, because the covenant violates his First Amendment right to the freedom of speech.

    b. Succeed, because the enforcement of the covenant would violate the Equal Protection Clause of the Fourteenth Amendment to the United States Constitution.

    c. Fail, because his conduct was seen by the children.

    d. Fail, because possession of pornography is a nuisance.

134. In September 1994, Oscar Ornithologist asked his neighbor Helga Habitat for permission to use her property to watch the annual migration of the spectacular but endangered whooping crane. Helga said that would be fine. One year later, Oscar asked Helga if he could use the land to watch the whooping cranes again, this time accompanied by a couple dozen members of the local Audubon Society. Again, Helga agreed. For the next several years, Oscar kept asking for permission to bring larger and larger groups onto the land, and Helga kept agreeing. Finally, on September 1, 2002, Oscar called Helga on her cell phone and asked her to allow the 5,000 participants in the Audubon Society's annual national convention to use her land for one week during each of the next five years. Helga said yes. Oscar then spent $100,000 of his own money to advertise the event and to secure non-refundable deposits for the few hotel rooms in the area. But on the day before the event, Helga changed her mind and refused to let anyone on her land. What property right do Oscar and the convention participants have with respect to Helga's land?

ANSWER:

135. Sally Adams lives in a house in Sycamore Woods, a new subdivision in a growing suburban area. It is the first house that she has ever owned. Sally had always wanted to plant rose bushes in front of her house, so she invited her new neighbor Beth to accompany her to the garden store to choose a dozen rose bushes. But Beth responded, "Sally, don't you know that flowers are not permitted in our front yards?" Sally and Beth dug out the paperwork containing the long list of covenants that were included on the deed to Sally's property, including a prohibition on "any flowering plants in the front yard of any property in this subdivision." Another provision in Sally's deed stated that "any violations of these covenants will be remedied by a judicial injunction as requested by the Sycamore Woods Homeowner's Association." Sally assumed that it would be easy to get permission to plant the rose bushes notwithstanding the covenant, but when she asked the president of the homeowner's association, he indicated that no exceptions were possible. Undeterred, Sally plans to file a lawsuit against the homeowner's association challenging the application of the covenant. Sally will:

a. Succeed because she did not have actual notice of the covenant.

b. Succeed because the homeowner's association lacks the authority to regulate her use of her property.

c. Fail because she is in horizontal privity with the homeowner's association.

d. Fail because the covenant is reasonable.

136. Growth controls serve each of the following purposes *except:*

    a. Preserving the existing character of a community.

    b. Separating inconsistent residential and industrial uses.

    c. Limiting traffic, pollution, and other consequences of an increasing population.

    d. Limiting the demand for roads, sewers, and public services.

137. Phyllis Scala owns a vacant lot in the village of Shoreland. The lot was created in 1923 as a part of a subdivision in the area. The Scala family purchased the lot in 1958, before the zoning ordinances were in place. The family had always planned to build on the lot and consistently mowed and kept a fence on it. The property borders a tidal marsh to the northeast, and is situated between a cottage on the southern side and another vacant lot on the northwestern side. The lot is a narrow wedge shape measuring 50 feet at the street, 200 feet on its longest side, and with 107 feet of frontage abutting the marsh. It is larger than many of the surrounding lots in the neighborhood. In April 2013, Phyllis sought a variance to build a cottage on the lot to move into following her retirement. The provision in the Shoreland Zoning Ordinance from which Phyllis sought a variance provided that any building must be set back from the marsh at least seventy-five feet, which she sought to reduce to twenty-five feet. A representative of the Scala family asserted that if they received a variance, the proposed structure would be set back at a similar distance from the marsh as the other homes in the area. What is Scala's best argument for a variance?

    a. The tidal marsh is disappearing anyway because of climate change.

    b. Her family bought the lot before the town enacted its zoning law.

    c. She cannot use the property unless she receives a variance.

    d. The proposed cottage complies with all of the other requirements of the town's zoning law.

138. Library Associates purchased the building located at 404 King Street which was formerly the main branch of the Charleston County Public Library. The 404 King Street property is located across the street from the Old Citadel in the historic heart of Charleston, South Carolina. 404 King was split-zoned: approximately 60% of the building was zoned 3X, permitting a building on that site to be 105 feet tall. The interior of the building that lies towards the Old Citadel was zoned 55/30, meaning the height could not exceed 55 feet nor could it be less than 30 feet high. The Old Citadel is also zoned 55/30, and is now the site

of an Embassy Suites Hotel. All other properties along the 400 block of King Street are zoned 3X, meaning their maximum height is three times the distance from the facade of the building to the center of King Street. After Library Associates bought the 404 King property, the Charleston City Council voted 10-6 to rezone that entire property 3X, too. A lawsuit brought by a local historic preservation group challenging that rezoning will:

a. Succeed, because rezoning can only occur with at least a 2/3 vote.

b. Succeed, because the rezoning violates the National Historic Preservation Act.

c. Fail, because the city council had a legitimate reason for rezoning only the 404 King property.

d. Fail, because the ad coelom doctrine allows Library Associates to build as tall of a building as it likes.

139. Willacy County is a largely rural area immediately adjacent to South Padre Island in Texas. The only way to reach the island from the county is a bumpy trip that requires a four-wheel drive vehicle and knowledge of tides that can trap a motorist on the return trip. The county would like to build a bridge to the north part of the island in order to promote tourism, fishing, and beach visits. But that part of the island is owned by the Nature Conservancy, which manages a preserve there for endangered sea turtles. Alternately, the county could build a bridge to the south part of the island, but that is part of the Padre Island National Seashore that is federal public land governed by the National Park Service pursuant to the Wilderness Act. The county is most likely to succeed in:

a. Asserting an easement by necessity to build the bridge to the north part of the island.

b. Acquiring part of the Nature Conservancy's land by eminent domain.

c. Asserting a riparian right to build the bridge to the south part of the island.

d. Persuading the National Park Service to exclude part of the national seashore from the coverage of the Wilderness Act.

140. The National Trust of Historic Preservation's list of the most endangered places in the United States included the oldest surviving McDonald's restaurant in the United States, located in Downey, California. McDonald's had long planned to close the Downey restaurant because of weak sales and the absence of such profitable amenities as a drive-thru window and indoor seating, and then the restaurant suffered minor damage from an earthquake. The city wants to preserve the McDonald's, so it enacted an ordinance prohibiting McDonald's from tearing down the restaurant. That ordinance is:

a. A valid exercise of the state's police power.

b. An invalid attempt to take the property for a non-public use.

c. A taking under *Lucas*.

d. Preempted by federal law.

141. Local historic preservation laws often limit:

    a. The right to alienate property.

    b. The right to destroy property.

    c. The right to exclude.

    d. The right to possess.

142. Which of the following operates as an exception to a property owner's right to exclude?

    a. Awarding punitive damages for intentional trespasses.

    b. Growth controls.

    c. Public accommodations laws prohibiting discrimination on the basis of race.

    d. The Religious Land Use and Institutionalized Persons Act.

143. When is a zoning change most likely to be overturned as spot zoning?

    a. It is sought instead of a variance.

    b. It fails to conform to the comprehensive plan.

    c. It was approved by less than a supermajority of the zoning board.

    d. It benefits some people more than others.

144. Snowmobiling is prohibited in most national parks unless:

    a. The National Park Service finds that the enjoyment of snowmobiling outweighs the impact on a park's preservation.

    b. There are no endangered animals living in the park.

    c. The park is not designated as a wilderness area.

    d. Congress has authorized snowmobiling in the park.

145. The Baton Rouge Audubon Society owns and manages a nature preserve designed to restore native vegetation along the Gulf of Mexico. Several neighboring homeowners object that the preserve attracts insects and is a fire hazard, so Cameron Parish (the Louisiana equivalent of a county) enacted an ordinance that makes it unlawful for landowners to "fail to regulate the growth of or accumulation of grass, obnoxious weeds, or other deleterious or unhealthful growths." The Audubon Society's best argument against the application of the new ordinance to the preserve is that the ordinance:

    a. The ordinance is an improper effort to regulate aesthetics.

    b. The application of the ordinance constitutes a regulatory taking under *Lucas*.

    c. The preserve does not contain obnoxious weeds or other deleterious or unhealthful growths.

    d. The ordinance conflicts with the goals of the federal Wilderness Act.

146. A Sunoco gas station opened on the southeast corner of Pennsylvania and Main Street in 1948 in the Village of Whistling Pines. In 1954, the Ellyn's Glen subdivision was built in the area bordered by Pennsylvania Avenue on the north and Main Street on the west (in other words, the area with the gas station at its northwest corner). Twenty of the twenty-two lots in the subdivision contain covenants restricting the use of the land to single-family homes. Within a year, houses were built on all twenty-two lots except for one lot neighboring the gas station; that lot remained vacant. In 1960, the village enacted a zoning ordinance designating the area on all sides of the intersection of Pennsylvania and Main Street for apartments only. Now the gas station wants to expand onto the one remaining lot in the subdivision. Does the gas station have the legal authority to expand?

ANSWER:

147. "We grant considerable discretion to agencies on matters requiring a high level of technical expertise" best describes a court's role in reviewing the decisions of:

    a. The United States Forest Service.

    b. A local zoning board.

    c. A divorce property adjudication.

    d. A local government's decision to employ its eminent domain power.

148. In 1977, the Acme Iron & Metal Company purchased 10 acres of land in a residential neighborhood. The company used an old house on the property for its business offices. In 2008, the city changed the zoning of the neighborhood to exclude any commercial enterprises. Shortly afterward, the company moved its business offices to another site, and instead the company began to use those 10 acres of land to collect and sort scrap metal. The neighbors object that the sounds, dust, and sight of the company's activities are so bad that it is impossible for them to enjoy living in their homes. Who will prevail in the resulting lawsuit between the neighbors and the company?

ANSWER:

149. The Charles C. Deam Wilderness Area is located in the Hoosier National Forest in southern Indiana. Which activity is most likely to be permitted there?

    a. A children's lemonade stand to sell drinks to weary hikers.

b. A ride service that drives the elderly residents of a nearby town to see the wilderness area's famous views.

c. The reconstruction of a historic iron forge that was built by the first settlers in the area during the 1820s.

d. A high school reunion trip that takes 80 people on a seven-day backpacking and camping trip.

150. The Ames Shovel Shops complex, an eight-acre site comprising 15 granite and wood buildings dating from 1852 through 1928, is the central core of what many consider an outdoor museum of 19th-century American development. The iron-bladed shovels fabricated there by generations of the Ames family literally built America. They were critical elements of the California Gold Rush, the Civil War, and the building of the Transcontinental Railroad. But the old shop buildings are threatened by toxic wastes that have leaked onto the property from the adjacent industrial operations that closed years ago, so the National Trust for Historic Preservation listed the shops in April 2009 as one of America's most endangered historic sites. Which law is least likely to hold the neighboring landowner responsible for cleaning up the wastes that are threatening the shops?

a. The National Historic Preservation Act.

b. CERCLA.

c. State private nuisance law.

d. State trespass law.

151. Jim owns a lot that contains a small house that was built sometime in the late nineteenth century. Like the other houses on the block, Jim's house is only 10 feet from the street and sits on a quarter-acre lot. In 1927, the town enacted a zoning law that permitted only residential uses and requiring a 20-foot minimum setback. Jim wants to replace the old house on his property and build a much larger home for his growing family. Jim's new house would be larger than the 3,000 square-foot homes that are permitted by the zoning ordinance. Jim's plans will likely:

a. Succeed, because the house is a nonconforming use.

b. Succeed, because Jim is entitled to a variance.

c. Fail, because the application of the zoning law to Jim's planned house constitutes spot zoning.

d. Fail, because Jim has not suffered any undue hardship.

152. The Comprehensive Environmental Response Compensation and Liability Act (CERCLA) of 1980 is a federal statute that holds landowners liable for the cost of cleaning up hazardous wastes that are in danger of escaping from their property, even if the current landowner did not introduce the wastes to the property. The best common law analogy to such liability is found in:

    a. Private nuisance law.

    b. Public nuisance law.

    c. Trespass law.

    d. Negligence principles of tort law.

153. Which of the following actions is prohibited by the federal Endangered Species Act?

    a. Amelia accidentally steps on an insect that was believed to be extinct since the nineteenth century.

    b. Benjamin uses his lawnmower to cut a patch of flowers that the federal government has listed as endangered under the ESA.

    c. In order to build a porch onto the back of his house, Carlos cuts down a tree that contains a nest used by an endangered bird.

    d. DeDe shoots an endangered grizzly bear that was attacking her as she was resting on the hammock in her backyard.

154. The Islamic Center owns 50 acres of land in the town of Mount Davis. In 1990, the Islamic Center applied for a conditional use permit that would allow the construction of a mosque. The town granted the permit subject to the condition that the Islamic Center not build an elementary school on the property. By 2002, the Islamic Center was interested in building a soup kitchen on its property adjacent to the mosque. The neighboring residents opposed such a soup kitchen, though, explaining at a public hearing that several sites in other parts of the town would be more appropriate for a homeless shelter and that "there are already enough of these people around here anyway." The town denied a permit for the soup kitchen for the stated reason that "services for the homeless are best provided by local governmental authorities." The best claim for the Islamic Center's challenge to that decision relies upon:

    a. The limits of the police power in authorizing the application of zoning ordinances.

    b. The illegality of conditional rezoning.

    c. The federal Religious Land Use and Institutionalized Persons Act.

    d. The free exercise clause of the first amendment to the United States Constitution.

155. The village of Rico just enacted a new zoning ordinance. The zones established by that ordinance were selected by the village council for the sole purpose of improving the quality of life — and economic well-being — of Rico's mayor. Pursuant to the new zoning scheme, a quiet retirement community suddenly discovers that a huge regional shopping center is being built on what had been the park across the street. What is the best way for the angry residents of the retirement community to block the shopping center?

    a. Sue to enjoin the shopping center as a nuisance.

b. Contest the power of the village to enact any zoning laws.

c. File a takings case.

d. Petition to change the zoning ordinance by popular initiative.

156. The City of Butterscotch is concerned that the growing number of art galleries in its downtown area is "displacing other varieties of businesses to the detriment of the long-term health of the City." Therefore, the city council just amended its zoning ordinance to limit the number of art galleries that can locate in the city's downtown. Which party is most likely to successfully challenge the application of the new ordinance?

a. Anna's Arts, which has operated in Butterscotch since 1992, and now wants to expand its gallery by building on property that it purchased soon after the city council enacted its new ordinance.

b. Betty's Beauties, which has sold antique furniture in Butterscotch since 1998, and now plans to feature the paintings of local artists in its shop instead.

c. Anna and Betty are both likely to succeed because the regulation of art galleries is not a valid governmental interest under the police power.

d. Neither Anna nor Betty will succeed in their challenge to the application of the new ordinance.

157. In 1982, the City of Boca Raton enacted an ordinance that prohibits vertical grave markers on cemetery plots. A group of city residents who own vacant cemetery plots allege that the ordinance will interfere with their right to place religious decorations on the graves of their family members. Will the city residents succeed in their RLUIPA claim?

ANSWER:

158. The National Trust for Historic Preservation included the entire State of Vermont on its 2004 list of America's 11 Most Endangered Places. It did so because "WalMart is planning to saturate the state . . . with seven new mammoth mega-stores, each with a minimum of 150,000 square feet. . . . The likely result: degradation of the Green Mountain State's unique sense of place, economic disinvestment in historic downtowns, loss of locally-owned businesses, and an erosion of the sense of community that seems an inevitable by-product of big-box sprawl." What kind of regulation is *least* likely to be used to successfully prevent WalMart from building its proposed new stores in Vermont?

a. City zoning ordinances.

b. County growth control laws.

c. Vermont's state historic preservation statute.

d. The National Historic Preservation Act.

159. The Acme Telephone Company wants to build a cell phone tower on land neighboring the Happy Days Preschool. The school is worried that the electromagnetic waves emitted by the tower could interfere with the learning of the young children at the school. Their lawsuit citing their medical worries as a basis for stopping the tower from being built will:

    a. Succeed, it if states a trespass claim.

    b. Succeed, if it states a private nuisance claim.

    c. Fail, unless the local zoning ordinance prohibits cell phone towers to be built near a school because of the concern about the effects of electromagnetic waves.

    d. Fail, because of the federal Telecommunications Act.

160. Municipal zoning ordinances authorize variances in order to avoid applications of zoning law that would violate which constitutional provision?

ANSWER:

161. Before 2025, Pasco County must build more and larger roads to accommodate the inevitable increase in automobile traffic. The county thus enacted a "Right of Preservation Ordinance," which designates new "transportation corridors" to expand certain county highways. For most landowners, whose land is encroached by the transportation corridor but who have no plans to develop the land adjacent to the encroached land, the county will take the expanded right-of-way — when needed — by eminent domain. For other landowners whose land is encroached by the new transportation corridor but who plan to develop the remaining land that adjoins the encroachment, the Ordinance requires the county to deny the landowner's development permit and to forbid development of the land adjoining the new transportation corridor unless the landowner "dedicates" (conveys in fee simple) to the county — for free — the land within the new transportation corridor. May the county impose such a dedication requirement?

ANSWER:

162. Harry Whittington acquired Block 38 in Austin, Texas in 1981. Block 38 is located next to the Austin convention center and is used for surface parking. The city opened the convention center in 1992. A 1,100 space parking garage one block west of the west entrance to the convention center has 600 spaces to serve the convention center and 500 spaces for monthly leases. In 1998, Austin voters approved an expansion to the convention center to more than double its size, financed by an increase in the hotel tax. After the expansion, a feasibility study indicated a lack of hotel rooms in close proximity to the convention center. The city thus contracted with a private developer to build, own, and operate a project that will include an 800-room hotel, residential space, retail shops, and underground parking that could support the expanded convention center. The city looked at acquiring Block 38 or a vacant block three blocks south of Block 38, and then giving the property to the private developer. City staff considered but decided against cancelling the 500 leases in the existing garage near the west side of the convention center because it relied on the steady stream of income from the monthly leases and the garage and its elevator were not located near the new north entrance to the convention center. The city chose to try to acquire Block 38 because of its close proximity to the north convention center entrance. The city will be able to acquire Block 38 from Worthington and then give it to the private developer unless:

a. The New Campbell Supreme Court interprets its state constitution consistent with the United States Supreme Court's decision in *Kelo v. City of New London.*

b. The New Campbell Supreme Court interprets its state constitution consistent with the Michigan Supreme Court's decision in *County of Wayne v. Hathcock.*

c. The hotel and parking lot project are reserved for official government business.

d. Worthington refuses to sell.

163. The fair market value test for determining just compensation does not apply if:

a. The fair market value cannot be determined.

b. The property has a special value to its owner.

c. It would cost the owner more to replace the property.

d. The government cannot afford to pay the fair market value.

164. The National Park Service is acquiring land to expand Everglades National Park in southern Florida. One parcel of land that the Park Service wants to acquire is owned by Jules Labak. Ideally, Labak would like to keep his land, but otherwise he would like to receive as much compensation as possible. Labak's best argument is that:

a. The Park Service cannot force him to sell the property because it does not involve a public use.

b. The Park Service must compensate him for the cost of find similar replacement property.

c. The amount of compensation should be based upon the property's value for residential subdivisions that current zoning law allows Labak to build there.

d. Labak's property is valuable because it enables him to run a bird watching business.

165. In early 2004, the City of Brighton decided to build a new wastewater treatment plant in unincorporated Weld County. For several years thereafter, Brighton engaged in actions and communications with a group of landowners evidencing its intent to construct the treatment plant on the landowners' properties. In August 2009, negotiations were still unsuccessful, so the landowners sued alleging that the city's actions and inactions during the lengthy precondemnation period have deprived them of their right to alienate their properties. The landowners' suit will likely:

a. Succeed, because the government's actions have reduced the value of their properties.

b. Succeed, because the government may physically take the properties in the future.

c. Fail, because the properties still retain significant value.

d. Fail, because the right to alienation is not a recognized aspect of property rights.

166. In 1992, Air Pegasus entered into a 20-year lease of a heliport in Washington, D.C. After the September 11 terrorist attacks, the Federal Aviation Administration (FAA) barred aircraft from taking off from or landing at civilian airports in and around Washington, D.C.

Air Pegasus closed its business operations a year after the terrorist attacks because it could not operate from the leased property. Is Air Pegasus entitled to compensation under the takings clause?

a. Yes, because the government deprived Air Pegasus of all of the value of its property.

b. Yes, because the regulations operate as a physical seizure of Air Pegasus's property.

c. No, because Air Pegasus did not have a property right to operate in navigable airspace.

d. No, because Air Pegasus was engaged in a nuisance.

167. In a 2000 report, the District of Columbia Office of Planning found that "if George Washington University (GW) continues to purchase land outside the campus plan boundaries and the number of students living in the small, constrained Foggy Bottom community continues to increase, the residential community will reach a 'tipping point' where the Foggy Bottom community simply transforms into a 'University' area." Accordingly, the District of Columbia Board of Zoning Adjustment (BZA) enacted numerous zoning provisions designed to regulate the expansion of GW. But several people living near GW complain that the university's continued expansion has resulted in increased noise and traffic and is altering the character of the neighborhood. Accordingly, those neighbors have sued alleging that the BZA's failure to enforce its zoning regulations has resulted in a taking of their property for purposes of the Fifth Amendment. That takings claim will likely:

a. Succeed, because the government has physically invaded the plaintiffs' property.

b. Succeed, because the application of the zoning law resulted in an unconstitutional exaction.

c. Fail, because the city's denial of all economically viable use of the property is permitted when it is necessary to abate a nuisance.

d. Fail, based on a balancing of the three factors identified in *Penn Central*.

168. Peggy owns a Kentucky Fried Chicken restaurant on the corner of Tyler Road and Kellogg Street. In 2002, the city redesigned Kellogg Street to build an overpass over Tyler Road, so customers can no longer reach the restaurant directly from Kellogg Street. The restaurant's business has plummeted in half since then. Does the city owe just compensation to Peggy?

ANSWER:

169. Which government action is most likely to be judged a taking of Julia's property?

a. A federal Environmental Protection Agency order requiring the permanent installation of three groundwater monitoring wells on Julia's land because of concerns that the aquifer below her land had been contaminated by pesticide runoff from neighboring farms.

    b. A state historic preservation statute that prohibits Julia from building a master bedroom suite onto her nineteenth century home.

    c. A new county zoning amendment that designates Julia's land as residential, thus preventing Julia from realizing her longstanding plan to someday operate a bed and breakfast there.

    d. A city health department's order to destroy Julia's building because anthrax was found there.

170. Leanna owns 50 acres of land which she uses for an orange grove. The fair market value of the land is six million dollars, but the assessed value for the purposes of Leanna's property taxes is only two million dollars because the land is subject to a conservation easement held by the Farmland Trust. The federal government wants Leanna's land so that it can build a new interstate highway. How much is Leanna likely to receive as a just compensation award?

ANSWER:

FINAL EXAM QUESTIONS

PRACTICE FINAL EXAM

171. Carrie Whittemore wants to build a house that is larger than that permitted on her lot by local land use regulations. What should she do?

ANSWER:

172. After election day on November 7, 2012, Lisa Whittemore placed a "Romney for President" sign in her front yard. Soon thereafter, Lisa received a letter from her homeowner's association informing her that a covenant attached to her property prohibits political signs except during the month before election day. What is Lisa's best legal authority for her ability to keep her sign in her front yard?

ANSWER:

173. You own a house in the Eagle Nest residential development. It is your vacation house and you spend about six long weekends a year there; the rest of the time you rent the house to others. The Eagle Nest Homeowner's Association has just increased the monthly parking fee for nonresident owners (like you) to $75 per month. Resident owners still pay the old fee of $25 per month. When you ask the homeowner's association why it adopted the new fee, it explains that it wants to prevent nonresident owners from realizing a profit by renting out their parking spaces to tenants at market rates. Is the homeowner's association's $75 per month parking fee for nonresidents valid?

ANSWER:

174. Tempe, Arizona's zoning ordinance requires that all commercial signs be colored turquoise, magenta, or white. The ordinance is intended to achieve a uniform appearance consistent with the southwestern architecture in the city. Blockbuster Video wants to open a store in Tempe using its traditional blue, yellow, and white signs. The city refuses to grant Blockbuster a variance or any other exception to the colors rule, so Blockbuster sues in court. Can Tempe enforce its ordinance against Blockbuster?

ANSWER:

175. Arthur just took the bar exam. He is sure that he has failed. So sure, in fact, that he told his classmate Charlie that Charlie could have the new laptop that Arthur planned to use in his law practice. Arthur explains that the laptop is being shipped from the manufacturer and should arrive at his home in three days. One day later, though, Arthur was killed in a

car accident. Charlie asked Arthur's heirs for the laptop, but they refused to give it to him. Does Charlie own the laptop?

ANSWER:

176. In what ways is one's vote for President property, and in what ways is it not property?

ANSWER:

177. Some courts have held that a landowner has a natural law right to the rainfall that occurs naturally upon that property, a right that cannot be violated by human weather modification activities. How would weather modification programs fare under other theories of property?

ANSWER:

178. Why is a physician exempt from a conversion claim when she removes body parts from a patient during a routine surgical procedure and then keeps them for later use in medical research?

ANSWER:

179. Alabama is one of the few states that fails to recognize an implied warranty of habitability. The state's supreme court has explained that "while we could recognize an implied warranty of habitability, as the tenant requests, we are of the opinion that the best forum for making a change in our law is the legislature." What is the best response that justifies judicial establishment of such an implied warranty?

ANSWER:

180. The Friendly General Store and the First Baptist Church own adjoining lots in the center of town. In 1944, the church built a new building for its growing congregation. In 1980, the general store began experiencing problems arising from leaking water, which the store soon traced to water falling from the overhanging gutters of the church. A survey of the lands determined that the roof of the church extends four feet across the boundary between the land owned by the parties. Is the church liable for a trespass?

ANSWER:

181. Before it was chased by Post and was killed by Pierson, who owned the fox in *Pierson v. Post*?

a. Pierson.

b. Post.

c. The owner of the land where the fox lived.

d. No one.

182. Assuming that Sue, Melissa, Amanda, Gloria, and Jack are each living, and none of the stated conditions have occurred yet, which of Jack's interests is invalid under the Rule against Perpetuities?

    a. Sue conveys her land "to Melissa for life, then to Jack, but if Jack ever opens a bed and breakfast, then to Amanda."

    b. Sue conveys her land "to Melissa so long as Melissa has child or grandchild who practices medicine, then to Jack."

    c. Sue conveys her land "to Melissa for life, then to Amanda if she graduates from college, then to Jack."

    d. Sue conveys her land "to Melissa for life, then to Amanda if Amanda survives Gloria, and otherwise to Jack."

183. In 1872, David Brewer inherited the fee simple absolute title to hundreds of acres of land in the northernmost part of Indiana. Upon his death in 1908, Brewer devised "my interest in a thirty-foot-wide strip of land running from the South Bend to Chicago to the Granger, Mishawka, and South Bend Railroad (GMSB)." What interest did GMSB receive from Brewer?

    a. Fee simple absolute.

    b. Fee simple determinable.

    c. Fee simple subject to a condition subsequent.

    d. An easement.

184. Dalton Edward Craigen left a holographic will that in its entirety stated: "Last Will & testament. I want Debbie to have everything till she dies. Being of sound mind & this is my last will & testament. I leave to my Wife Daphne Craigen all real & personal property. I want my Wife to share all of my property with my Children." It turns out the "Debbie" and "Daphne Craigen" is the same person. The will is obviously ambiguous, but which of the following results is least likely to occur?

    a. Dalton's wife (whether we call her Debbie or Daphne) owns all of the property in fee simple.

    b. Dalton's wife owns a life estate, and Dalton's children have a vested remainder.

    c.   Dalton's children own all of the property in fee simple absolute.

    d.   Dalton's wife and Dalton's children own the property as tenants in common.

185. In the early morning hours of December 17, 2010, the Huntington Police Department (HPD) received an anonymous child welfare call reporting that children were in a home with drugs and guns at 525 30th Street in Huntington, West Virginia. At around 4:00 am, several HPD officers went to the 525 30th Street residence, knocked on the door, and were permitted to enter by Patrick Wiles, one of the tenants. The officers told Wiles they were there in response to a child welfare call, and asked to look around the residence. Wiles assented, but his roommate Terence McArthur objected. The HPD officers proceeded to search the entire resident, and they found heroin hidden in a Santa Claus hat on the shelf in the closet in McArthur's bedroom, and they charged McArthur with possession of illegal drugs. McArthur's best argument against the legality of the search is that:

    a.   McArthur and Wiles owned the property as joint tenants.

    b.   McArthur and Wiles owned the property as tenants in common.

    c.   McArthur objected to the search.

    d.   The police need the consent of all cotenants in order to search a home.

186. Judge Bruce Wilkins wrote the following passage in a 2004 case: "Much like Scotland's famous Loch Ness monster, the Plaintiffs' 'deep, deep contaminant plume' is believed to be 'down there somewhere,' and has not been conclusively proven not to exist, but its proponents have yet to come forward with significant probative admissible evidence of specific facts affirmatively demonstrating that it does exist." The plaintiffs are most likely to:

    a.   Succeed in their private nuisance claim, but not their trespass claim.

    b.   Succeed in their trespass claim, but not their private nuisance claim.

    c.   Succeed in both their private nuisance and trespass claims.

    d.   Fail in both their private nuisance and trespass claims.

187. The continuing validity of the ad coelom doctrine is best illustrated by:

    a.   Claims that the installation of cable television wires is outside the scope of an existing easement.

    b.   The traditional rules governing trespass claims against air pollution that interferes with a beachfront landowner's view of the sunset.

    c.   State regulation of groundwater pumping.

    d.   The rules governing treasure troves.

188. You own land that is next to an old factory. There is no evidence of any contamination on your property, or even at the factory itself, but many people in the neighborhood believe that your land is contaminated. You would like to sell your land, and Julia wants to buy it "as is." What are you most likely to have to tell Julia before she buys the land?

    a. That there is no evidence of any contamination on your property.

    b. That your neighbors believe that your land is contaminated.

    c. Both (a) and (b).

    d. Neither (a) nor (b).

189. Harold bought a unit in the New Phoenix Atlantic Condominiums in 1984. He decided to use parking space number 32, which he did regularly until 1999, when the condominiums reconfigured the parking lot and reduced the size of parking space number 32. In the resulting lawsuit against the condominiums, Harold will likely establish:

    a. Fee simple title to the parking space.

    b. An easement by estoppel.

    c. An easement by prescription.

    d. No property right to the parking space.

190. Mr. and Mrs. Gonzalez own an easement to walk across their neighbor Anita's land to the beach. Four years ago, the path became impassable as a result of subsidence caused by another neighbor's excessive groundwater pumping. Since then, Mr. and Mrs. Gonzalez have used a different path across Anita's land to reach the beach, but Anita objects because the path is too close to her vegetable garden. If the parties litigate their dispute, Mr. and Mrs. Gonzelez will:

    a. Win, because their use the new path across Anita's land does not impose an additional burden on Anita.

    b. Win, because they now have a prescriptive easement to use the new path across Anita's land.

    c. Lose, because of the majority rule concerning the relocation of easements.

    d. Lose, because the new route to the beach is not within the scope of permissible activities under the easement.

191. Ron Nichols and the City of Evansdale owned properties six blocks away from each other until 2011, when they exchanged parcels. The city wanted to build a new road across the property that had been owned by Nichols, while Nichols wanted to build three homes on the land that had been owned by the city. After the transfer, Nichols learned that he could not build on his new property because the city's sewer lines across that property interfered with any possible construction. Nichols responded by suing the city. The most likely result

of the lawsuit is that the city:

a. Has a prescriptive easement to maintain the sewer lines upon the property now owned by Nichols.

b. Has an easement by implication to maintain the sewer lines upon the property now owned by Nichols. *prior use?*

c. May keep the sewer lines where they are because Nichols does not have a property interest in the area beneath the surface of his land.

d. Is liable for a trespass.

192. In 1956, Fred Cline began operating a fertilizer business and junk yard on land that he owned in the town of Abingdon. In 1967, the town enacted a new zoning ordinance that zoned Cline's property as single family residential, and which further provided that all uses not expressly permitted within a particular district are prohibited. In 1968, Cline asked the town to rezone his property to allow his expanding business, but he later dropped that request. Then, in 1995, Terry Bell bought the land from Cline and continued to operate the junk yard. May Bell operate the junk yard?

a. Yes, provided that Bell also lives in a home on the property.

b. Yes, because it is a nonconforming use.

c. No, because Bell does not also operate a fertilizer business.

d. No, because a nonconforming use expires after 30 years.

193. The City of Dordt wants to buy land for its mayor to use as a luxury retirement home once he leaves office. It will mostly likely be able to do so if:

a. The mayor reimburses the city for the use of eminent domain.

b. The city's voters authorize the use of eminent domain in a public referendum.

c. The current owner of the land agrees to sell it to the city.

d. None of the above.

194. RIHR Incorporated, owner of two residential development lots in Carrollton, Texas, applied to the City of Carrollton for building permits to complete construction of houses on those lots. The city conditioned its issuance of those permits on RIHR's payment of the cost of rebuilding a collapsed retaining wall used to prevent flooding in the neighborhood. RIHR's lawsuit against the city will:

a. Succeed, if the collapsed wall was on another lot owned by someone else.

b. Succeed, if the public will not be allowed to use the repaired wall.

c. Fail, if RIHR knew about the collapse of the wall.

d. Fail, if the wall is necessary to safeguard the neighborhood from flooding resulting from RIHR's new houses.

195. The relationship between the federal Telecommunications Act and local zoning law is most similar to the relationship between which other federal statute and local zoning law:

a. The Clean Water Act's wetlands provisions.

b. The Comprehensive Environmental Restoration, Cleanup and Liability Act.

c. The Endangered Species Act.

d. The Religious Land Use & Institutionalized Persons Act.

196. The public trust doctrine presupposes:

a. The government's power of eminent domain.

b. The ability of the government to obtain land by adverse possession.

c. Original government ownership of land within a state.

d. The government's ability to use its police power to protect environmental resources.

197. Whether or not a government land use regulation "goes too far" determines whether that regulation:

a. Constitutes a regulatory taking requiring just compensation.

b. Constitutes an exaction.

c. Violates the Rule against Perpetuities.

d. Preempts state nuisance law liability.

198. Congress is concerned that federal agencies are failing to develop adequate web sites that describe the government's work to the public. Congress is also loathe to compete with the salaries offered to web designers in the private sector. Accordingly, Congress enacts a statute authorizing agencies to use the web sites of private corporations as models for federal agency web sites. Soon thereafter, the Department of Agriculture's new web site bears an uncanny resemblance to the web site of the American Farm Association (AFA). The AFA's takings claim against the federal government will:

a. Succeed, because the federal government has used the AFA's web site without permission.

b. Succeed, because of the congressional purpose to avoid having to hire web designers.

c. Fail, because web site designs are not property within the meaning of the takings clause

    d. Fail, because the AFA's web site still retains substantial value.

199. Which of the following cases illustrates the denominator problem?

    a. Alicia's Market purchased 20 acres of forested land in 1990, built a store on 10 acres in 1996, used seven more acres to add to the store in 1999, and is now told by the city that it cannot build on the last three acres of land because a rare salamander has just been sighted there.

    b. The Benjamin Realty Company owns 50 acres of undeveloped land that it has been hoping to use for a shopping center, but it just learned that the entire property qualifies as wetlands that cannot be developed without a permit, and the state refuses to issue a permit for a shopping center there.

    c. In 2001, the Community Church was received a gift of 100 acres so that the church could expand its ministries. The city now wants to exercise its eminent domain power so that the 100 acres can be used for a large public recreational facility.

    d. Dr. Davis acquired 10 acres in 2000, and she is now told by the state that she can only develop five acres if she sets aside the other five acres as wildlife habitat.

200. Rob and Jerry have owned neighboring houses in New Rochelle since 1962. Soon after they purchased their properties, they discovered that the lengthy circular driveway that runs between their houses was in fact located entirely on Rob's property. Jerry then purchased an easement from Rob "to use the driveway for ingress and egress to Jerry's property." Over the years, Jerry planted two dozen cherry trees alongside the part of the driveway nearest his house. The trees were on the part of Rob's property across which Jerry had an easement. But after Rob moved and sold his property to Lou in 1998, Lou took out his chain saw and prepared to cut down the cherry trees. Jerry's suit to block Lou from cutting the trees will:

    a. Succeed because Jerry has an express easement that gives him the right to keep the trees.

    b. Succeed because Jerry has a prescriptive easement that gives him a right to keep the trees.

    c. Succeed because Jerry has both an express easement and a prescriptive easement that give him a right to keep the trees.

    d. Fail because Jerry has neither an express easement nor a prescriptive easement that gives him a right to keep the trees.

201. In 1989, Jim and Dawn built houses on adjacent properties. State Route 10 — the only nearby highway — borders Jim's land on the west, and Dawn's property borders Jim's land on the east, so Dawn wants to be able to cross Jim's land to reach her land. Her claim to an easement by necessity will always fail if:

    a. Dawn had offered to buy an express easement from Jim, but he refused.

b. The land now owned by Jim and Dawn was never owned by a single person.

c. Patricia owned all of the land now owned by Jim and Dawn until 1944, when she sold one lot to Jim and another lot to Dawn because Patricia disliked all of the traffic that the new Route 10 had generated.

d. Dawn could reach her property by spending $700,000 to build a fifteen-mile private road across the mountains to the east of her land that connects to a dirt road that is usually open to the public.

202. According to the terminology of Professors Calabresi and Malamed, state statutes that prevent farming operations from being challenged as nuisances are examples of:

a. A plaintiff protected by a property rule.

b. A plaintiff protected by a liability rule.

c. A defendant protected by a property rule.

d. A defendant protected by a liability rule.

203. Which party is most likely to be able to keep the most of the goods that she made?

a. Anna, who watched a meteor fall from the sky onto her neighbor's backyard, ran over and took it, and used the stone to make several dozen inexpensive necklaces.

b. Betty, who snuck into her neighbor's stream, panned for gold, melted the gold dust that she found, and crafted a small ring.

c. Celia, who accidentally mixed the grapes that she harvested from her vineyard with grapes that she accidentally harvested from her neighbor's land, and then produced an award-winning wine.

d. Daphne, who got lost in the woods behind her house and accidentally wandered onto her neighbor's land, found an empty turtle shell, brought it home and painted it blue, and gave it to her six-year-old daughter to play with as a toy.

204. Which landlord is most likely to regain possession of his property from the current tenant?

a. Allen, who declined to renew his tenant Anthony's apartment lease for a tenancy at will when Allen discovered that Anthony had posted complaints about the apartment on the city housing department's web site.

b. Bryce, who leased farmland to Boyd for one year based on Boyd's local reputation as an excellent hog farmer, and who objects to Boyd's plan to sublease the property to a college friend who wants to live in the country for a while.

c. Carla, who leased a house to Chris with explicit notice of the house's many failings, and who now seeks to evict Chris, who refuses to pay the rent until Celia fixes the pipes to provide water to the home.

    d. Deborah, who rented office space to David, a doctor who refuses to pay the rent because the noise from the city hospital next door makes it impossible for him to work there.

205. Which of the following acts is permitted by the Fair Housing Act?

    a. A suburban family refuses to rent its house to a man because the man is from China.

    b. A developer refuses to rent an apartment to a white college student because the developer wants to maintain a racially integrated building.

    c. An apartment owner advertises in a local newspaper indicating that only women will be considered to live in vacant units.

    d. A developer refuses to sell a house in a new subdivision that he has just constructed to an Episcopal priest because the developer wants to create a community that is comprised of 100 Jewish families.

206. Shortly after they were married, George and Sylvia purchased a house in New Campbell as tenants by the entirety. Ten years later, they agreed to live apart for a while to see if they could work out their differences. Sylvia continued to live in the house. Before George moved out, Sylvia told him that they should sell the house and divide the proceeds equally if they could not reconcile their marriage. Sylvia died in a car accident five weeks after George moved out. Her will devised all of her property to her sister Betsy. Who owns what interest in the house?

    a. George owns the house in fee simple absolute.

    b. Betsy owns the house in fee simple absolute.

    c. George and Betsy own the house as tenants in common.

    d. George and Betsy own the house as joint tenants.

207. Melinda and Brandon are getting a divorce after 12 years of marriage. They have two significant assets: a mutual fund which contains the income that Brandon earned and which is now worth $300,000, and a $60,000 car that was a gift to Brandon from his parents five years ago. In a community property state, Melinda is most likely entitled to:

    a. An equitable distribution of the mutual fund and value of the car.

    b. Neither the car nor the mutual fund.

    c. $180,000.

    d. An equal distribution of the mutual fund.

208. In 1990, Alice and Gerald were married. Ten years later, they purchased a vacation home as tenants by the entirety. But Gerald soon lost his lucrative job managing a global mutual fund when the stock market lost much of its value. Gerald was desperate to fend off his

creditors, so he sold them his interest in the vacation home. One month later, Gerald died, devising all of his property to his children. What interest do Gerald's creditors have in the vacation home?

a. They own it in fee simple.

b. They own it as tenants in common with Alice.

c. They own it as tenants in common with Alice and with Gerald's children.

d. They do not have any interest in it.

209. Frank and Joseph lived together as a gay couple in a house they bought as tenants in common. Ten months ago, their relationship ended and Frank moved out of the house. Frank has since conveyed his interest in the house to Kelly, who is a local real estate agent. Kelly wants to sell the house, but Joseph would rather keep it. Kelly will:

a. Be able to sell the house because an out-of-possession owner has superior rights to the possessing owner.

b. Be able to sell the house as the result of a partition action.

c. Not be able to sell the house because Joseph obtained the fee simple title to the house when Frank tried to sell it.

d. Not be able to sell the house if Joseph pays Kelly rent for living there.

210. In February 2000, the Axle Motor Company conveyed its riverfront property "to Lucy Brewer for life, then to her eldest daughter." At the time of the conveyance, Lucy had two daughters: Annie, age 16; and Tanya, age 12. Two years later, when she turned 18, Annie conveyed her interest in the land to the Prairie Land Trust. At the same time, Lucy leased the property "to Dean Walter for five years." In January 2003, Lucy and Annie died in a car accident. Who is most likely to have the possessory interest in the land following the fatal accident?

a. The Axle Motor Company.

b. The Prairie Land Trust.

c. Tanya.

d. Dean Walter.

211. Jane McCartney has given land to each of her children when they got married. Her youngest daughter Julie is not married, but she has been living with Henry for five years, and they have two children together. So, in 2001, Jane conveyed 10 acres "to Julie and Henry as tenants by the entirety, but if they ever get divorced, then to Julie." In 2003, Julie and Henry got married. Upon her marriage, one of the interests that Julie owns in the land is:

a. A tenancy by the entirety.

b. A joint tenancy or a tenancy in common, depending upon the jurisdiction.

c. A contingent remainder.

d. A springing executory interest.

212. The Mountain Realty Company conveyed 10 acres of land "to Elaine for life." Two years later, Elaine drafted a will devising all of her property to her son Randy. Then Randy sold his interest in the land "to Sara so long as she does not allow a SUV to enter the property." Next Elaine sold the land "to the county for use as a park." Finally, Elaine died. Who owns the possessory interest in the 10 acres of land?

a. Mountain Realty Company.

b. Randy.

c. Sara.

d. The county.

213. The Danish band Aqua recorded the song "Barbie Doll," which soon became an international hit. Alas, Mattel — the toy manufacturer that produces Barbie dolls — was not amused. Mattel failed to block Aqua from performing the song in concert, though, for each reason except:

a. The copyright law does not apply to live performances.

b. The song did not constitute trademark infringement because it did not suggest that it was created by Mattel.

c. The first amendment restricts government regulation of the song because the song is not purely commercial speech.

d. The song satisfied the noncommercial use exception of the Federal Trademark Dilution Act.

214. Commercial sperm banks are subject to little government regulation because:

a. Human body parts cannot be treated as property.

b. The state's police power may not be employed to regulate any aspects of human reproduction.

c. Few state legislatures have approved such regulation.

d. Any public concerns about such facilities are adequately addressed by private consensual agreements between the facilities and the donors.

215. The "fair use" provision of the federal copyright act presumes that:

a. Ideas cannot become property.

b. Monopoly power over written works is contrary to the public interest.

c. There is a natural right to use written works for noncommercial purposes.

d. Written works retain their commercial value for a short period of time.

216. Samuel wanted to thank Kelly, his employee, for landing a lucrative government contract. Samuel thus wrote a letter stating as follows: "In recognition of extraordinary effort, I am hereby giving Kelly my antique quill pen that was once used by Thomas Jefferson." The pen itself, Samuel explained, was on display in the building's lobby, and he told Kelly to meet him in his office tomorrow morning to receive the pen itself. One of Kelly's colleagues, Omar, overheard the conversation and entered Samuel's office after Kelly left. "Thomas Jefferson is a distant relative," Omar explained to Samuel, "and I will pay you $50,000 for that pen." Samuel agreed, accepted Omar's check for $50,000, and promised to give him the pen tomorrow morning. The next morning, Kelly arrived early and explained his situation to the building's custodian, who then opened the display case and gave Kelly the pen. Who owns the pen?

a. Samuel.

b. Kelly.

c. Omar.

d. Thomas Jefferson's heirs.

217. Jeff is a law student whose laptop computer was broken. He took the computer to We Fix It, a local store that is popular with students both because of its ability to solve any computer problem and because it offers used computers for sale at low prices. Two days later, Monica saw the computer on display at We Fix it and bought it. Monica did not know that the computer was Jeff's until she brought it home from the store and a mutual friend recognized the picture of Jeff's family that served as the wallpaper for the computer. Who owns the computer?

a. Jeff, because he was the original owner.

b. Jeff, because We Fix It did not act in good faith.

c. Monica, because We Fix It had voidable title.

d. Monica, because We Fix It has void title.

218. H.M. Chaney owned a $23,514.70 certificate of deposit. When he became sick, he wrote the following on the back of the certificate: "Pay to Martin, but not until my death. My life seems to be uncertain. I may live through this spell. Then I will attend to it myself." Chaney delivered the certificate to Martin and died two weeks later without recovering from his sickness. Martin's suit to cash the certificate will:

    a. Succeed, because it is a valid gift causa mortis.

    b. Succeed, because Chaney actually delivered the certificate to Martin.

    c. Fail, because the death of the donor cannot be a precondition to the validity of the gift.

    d. Fail, because Chaney did not satisfy the delivery requirement.

219. Which business is most likely to be liable to Julia if it loses the goods that she left with it?

    a. You Park It, which allowed Julia to park her car on its land near the airport.

    b. The First National Bank, which kept Julia's antique watch in a safe deposit box.

    c. Jose's Parking Lot, which allowed Julia to park her car in its enclosed garage without knowing that she had an expensive Ming dynasty vase in a box in the trunk.

    d. The Hillis Department Store, where Julia accidentally left her purse containing $2,000 in cash.

220. Which of the following can be established implicitly rather than explicitly?

    a. A tenancy at will.

    b. A real covenant.

    c. A homeowner's association's recreational fee.

    d. A zoning variance.

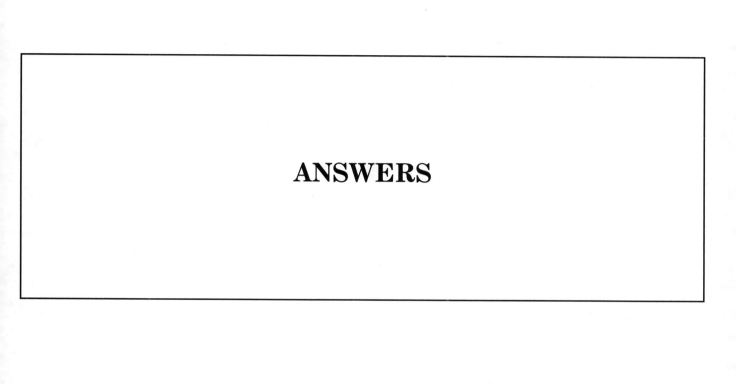

ANSWERS

1. **Answer (A) is the correct answer.** Ownership of oil and gas usually depends on title to the surface estate. Occupation of the surface of the land includes ownership of the oil and gas underneath the land as well. The capture theory is slightly different insofar as it requires the actual possession of the oil and gas, but it too emphasizes the ownership of the surface estate.

    Answer (B) is incorrect because the riparian doctrine that applies to water in the eastern United States only provides right of use, not actually ownership of the water. **Answer (C) is incorrect** because trademark law focuses on the labor used to create a brand rather than the occupation of an existing symbol. **Answer (D) is incorrect** because human body parts, to the extent they are viewed as property, depend on an idea of natural rights instead of the idea that one "occupies" one's own body.

2. There is no freestanding body of cultural property in the United States. The common law of property has yet to recognize cultural property. Instead, cultural property arises from notions of moral rights that the legislation may (or may not) decide to protect with specific statutes. Additionally, in most instances cultural property operates as a limit on other kinds of private property rights. For example, while the owner of a written scroll usually has a broad range of rights with respect to that property, the designation of that scroll as cultural property operates to limit the private owner's rights in favor of the holder of the cultural property claim.

3. **Answer (A) is the correct answer.** Riparian water rights give the owner of the land adjoining the water the right to use that water. Riparian rights do not confer actual ownership of the water. The water in a river or lake is ordinarily governed by the state as a matter of the public trust.

    Answer (B) is incorrect because a business that has a trade secret actually owns that trade secret in the eyes of the law. **Answer (C) is incorrect** because a successful adverse possession claim takes title to the property from the original owner and gives that title to the adverse possessor. **Answer (D) is incorrect** because the rule of capture applicable to oil and gas enables the party to capture the resource to own it.

4. **Answer (B) is the correct answer.** The occupation theory awards ownership of property to the person who possesses it. The court in *Willcox* recited the aphorism that "possession is nine-tenths of the law." There was no certain evidence of how Willcox came into possession or how any other party was dispossessed, so the fact that Willcox possessed the letters made him the owner.

    Answer (A) is incorrect because natural law looks for a fundamental moral justification for awarding property rights, and Willcox's mere possession did not offer any such claim. **Answer (C) is incorrect** because a utilitarian theory involves a societal balancing of interests which the court refused to consider when it simply relied on Willcox's possession of the letters. **Answer (D) is incorrect** because the possession of the letters did not require any labor by Willcox, who did not even know that he had them until he went through his grandmother's attic.

5.   **Answer (D) is the correct answer.** An anticommons is a resource with many owners, each of whom has the power to prevent others from using it, thus potentially frustrating the use of the resource in a way that would be most socially beneficial. A biotechnology (or other) invention that has many different components is likely to have many different owners of those components, thanks to the ability to patent each separate component and not just the whole. Each patent owner will have a veto power over the use of the whole invention.

    Answer (A) is incorrect because grazing on national forest lands is an example of the tragedy of the *commons* — not the anticommons — for it presents the opposite problem of each user being unable to limit the activities of other users, to the detriment of the entire resource. **Answer (B) is incorrect** because zoning law does not necessarily apply to land owned by multiple parties, so the zoning restrictions are independent of each owner's desires. **Answer (C) is incorrect** because the writer of a song enjoys copyright protection to exclude anyone else from using it (subject to fair use).

6.   **Answer (B) is the correct answer.** The utilitarian theory of property posits that whether or not something qualifies as property depends entirely on the judgment of the law. In Bentham's words, "Property is nothing but a basis of expectation." The federal Visual Artists Rights Act, by contrast, presumes that artists possess natural rights that exist prior to the societal determination to describe them as property.

    Answer (A) is incorrect because the utilitarian theory suggests that people should be able to use wilderness areas, contrary to the Wilderness Act. **Answer (C) is incorrect** because the so-called "arbitrary community judgment" is in fact the kind of balancing of needs that the utilitarian theory embraces. **Answer (D) is incorrect** because contract law principles reflecting the agreement between the parties are not inconsistent with the utilitarian theory, and are actually likely to be consistent with that theory based on each party's assessment of the best use of the property.

7.   **Answer (A) is the correct answer.** The owner of a patent holds the property rights to her invention, including the right to destroy. Patent law does not impose any obligation that a patent holder actually use an invention. Nor does patent law prohibit an inventor from destroying her invention.

    Answer (B) is incorrect because many jurisdictions have laws protecting famous works of art from destruction. **Answer (C) is incorrect** because state and local historic preservation laws often prohibit a landowner from destroying an historic building. **Answer (D) is incorrect** because anti-cruelty laws make it illegal to kill or otherwise destroy a pet animal, such as a cat.

8.   **Answer (C) is the correct answer.** Avulsion refers to the sudden loss or addition to land resulting from water adding or taking away the land. Property law awards the new land to — or takes the washed away land from — the owner of the property subject to avulsion. The effects of avulsion operate independently of the actions of the property owner; they do not depend on capture.

Answer (A) is incorrect because a wild animal can be reduced to ownership by capture. Likewise, **Answer (B) is incorrect** because some jurisdictions apply the capture rule to determine ownership of natural gas. **Answer (D) is incorrect** because many jurisdictions apply the rule of capture to acquiring ownership of groundwater.

9.   **Answer (B) is the correct answer.** The tragedy of the anticommons occurs when multiple owners each have the power to prevent others from using it. Mayor Goodman's insistence that he will oppose the Stratosphere if anyone in the neighborhood objects to it exemplifies that tragedy.

Answer (A) is incorrect because it occurs when multiple owners harm the land by too much use, not by too little use. **Answer (C) is incorrect** because the labor theory teaches that property rights should depend on the work that one has done to establish the value of the property, which does not really describe the concern of the neighbors. **Answer (D) is incorrect** because Mayor Goodman's deference to the neighbors is not grounded in any suggestion that they have a natural right to exclude unwanted projects such as the Stratosphere.

10.   **Answer (A) is the correct answer.** The Visual Artists Rights Act of 1990 (VARA) seeks to implement the moral rights to artwork that were originally recognized in European states, especially France. Those moral rights exist independent regardless of the law's recognition of them. VARA is a congressional effort to recognize those natural rights in a federal statute.

Answer (B) is incorrect because VARA actually restricts the authority of landowners to use their property. **Answer (C) is incorrect** because VARA applies only during the life of the artist, which is consistent with the constitutional direction that intellectual property rights be of a *limited* duration. **Answer (D) is incorrect** because VARA protection to "modification of a work of recognized stature," which directs the law to rely on social judgment about the stature of a work.

11.   **Answer (A) is the correct answer.** The law of avulsion states that land which is added to waterfront property as the result of a sudden action such as a hurricane or an earthquake does not become the property of the riparian owner. Instead, land added by avulsion belongs to the government. This is so even though the riparian landowner is likely to have treated the new land exactly like the preexisting land, by possessing them both alike.

Answer (B) is incorrect because land created by accretion does belong to the riparian owner. Accretion results from the gradual, imperceptible addition of land to the waterfront property already owned by the riparian owner. Possession does produce ownership in such circumstances. **Answer (C) is incorrect** because the law of accession, which addresses property that has been accidentally confused or mixed together, determines ownership based upon the equitable circumstances of particular cases. Possession may result in ownership of property obtained by accession, but it may not, too. **Answer (D) is incorrect** because adverse possession is the best illustration of the law determining ownership based upon possession, even possession that displaces the original owner.

12.   Utilitarian theory posits that the idea of property is a human construction that depends solely upon societal needs. Clay's remark captures that idea precisely. None of the other traditional theories of property fit Clay's statement. Natural rights theory insists that property exists independent of any given society's declarations. Nor does labor theory apply

for Clay's statement ignores any role that human labor plays in creating that which the law regards as property. Clay's statement of the nature of property does not contain an economic component, either.

13. **Answer (C) is the correct answer.** The public accommodations provisions of state civil rights statutes limit the ability of landowners to exclude certain members of the public from hotels, restaurants, and the like. By contrast, **Answer (A) is incorrect** because the federal trademark act gives a trademark holder the exclusive right to use a trademark, and anyone else's unlicensed use of the mark constitutes trademark infringement. **Answer (B) is incorrect** because state riparian rights to water extend to riparian owners of the waterbody, and those owners are entitled to exclude anybody whose actions would interfere with those rights. **Answer (D) is incorrect** because municipal historic preservation ordinances restrict the modification of historic properties, but such ordinances do not limit the ability of the property's owner to exclude others.

14. **Answer (B) is the correct answer.** The public trust doctrine teaches that some property is of such importance that the public retains a trust to the land. Private owners may acquire land subject to the public trust doctrine, but the owner will own the land subject to the rights of the public to use it or to protect it from certain harms. For example, the New Jersey courts have held that beachfront property is subject to the public trust doctrine so that a private owner of such property cannot exclude the public from crossing it to get to the beach. *See Matthews v. Bay Head Improvement Ass'n*, 471 A.2d 355 (N.J.), *cert. denied*, 469 U.S. 821 (1984). The public trust doctrine thus conforms to the scriptural indication that landowners should be willing to let others use their land.

   Answer (A) is incorrect because a tenancy at sufferance is a leasehold estate that can be ended at any time (subject to notice requirements). A tenancy at sufferance allows a tenant to remain on the landlord's property after a formal lease has expired, but the tenancy does not seek to discourage the new leasehold if the landlord chooses to do so. **Answer (C) is incorrect** because the touch and concern requirement determines whether a covenant runs with the land, and such covenants refer to restrictions upon land use rather than a right to let others use the land. **Answer (D) is incorrect** because spot zoning prohibitions bear little relation to whether others will be allowed to use the affected land. Spot zoning often benefits a small parcel of land, and that benefit attaches to the landowner regardless of the owner's willingness to make the land available to others.

15. A casino that operates as a private business enjoys all of the property rights afforded to landowners. Perhaps the most important such right is the right to exclude others from one's property. A casino is also a place of public accommodation, but the traditional common law placed relatively few limits upon public accommodations. Now, however, a number of states have statutes that empower a licensed casino to regulate those who demonstrate what is judged an unfair ability to win at various games. Such regulations are plainly within the police power of the state, as demonstrated by the long line of cases describing various gaming activities as a public nuisance. None of the other sources of property law explain the card-counting rule. For example, zoning laws are unlikely to address questions such as the rights of casinos to exclude unwanted patrons. Also, while federal civil rights laws offer guarantees with respect to public accommodations, those guarantees are only offered to special categories of people whom the law protects from discrimination. Gamblers generally, and card-counters in particular, are not protected by federal civil rights laws.

16. Amy does not have a good legal argument that would entitle her to recovering her infant items. The best she can hope for is that the recipients of the gifts will in turn give them back to her, which would constitute an entirely new gift in the eyes of the law. The law only recognizes a very narrow group of conditional gifts (such as engagement rings), and even if a court was willing to expand that group, Amy did not expressly state that her gift was contingent on anything (such as her mistaken belief that she would not have any more children). Nor does the law require that gifts be in writing to be effective. The only three legal requirements for a gift are offer, acceptance, and delivery, each of which was accomplished in this case before Amy changed her mind.

17. One with voidable title can transfer good title to a good faith purchaser who does not know of the rights of others, but one with void title cannot transfer good title even to a bona fide purchaser. Norwood voluntarily transferred possession of the heifers to Asbury, who thus acquired voidable title to them. Likewise, Hargrove later acquired voidable title from Asbury. Finally, when Maulsby acquired the heifers from Hargrove, Maulsby had no reason to think that Hargrove was not the true owner of the heifers. Maulsby thus qualifies as a bona fide purchaser who nows owns the heifers. Norwood's claim, while equitably appealing, loses to the rights of the bona fide purchaser. Moreover, Asbury's creditors have a lesser claim than both Maulsby and Norwood. And Hargrove gave up his right to the heifers when he sold them to Maulsby.

18. The First National Bank of Chicago never intentionally relinquished its claim to the certificates of deposit. The fact that the certificates were contained in the file cabinets was unknown to the bank. As the court explained in *Michael v. First Chicago Corp.*, 487 N.E.2d 403 (Ill. App. Ct. 1985), "Where both buyer and seller were ignorant of the existence or presence of the concealed valuable, and the contract was not broad enough to indicate an intent to convey all the contents, known or unknown, the courts have generally held that as between the owner and purchaser, title to the hidden article did not pass by the sale." The bank thus did not abandon the certificates, and it has the right to reclaim its property. By contrast, Zibton did not intend to buy the certificates, nor did the bank intend to sell them. Strayve's claim fails against the bank, which never intended to surrender its title to the certificates. Finally, a finder's claim fails against the true owner if that owner can be located.

19. As the court explained in *Hazen v. Best Buy Co.*, 2013 U.S. Dist. LEXIS 29590 (E.D. Mich. Mar. 4, 2013), "The bailment claim is based on the allegation that Best Buy was negligent in handling Hazen's property, i.e. the CDs which purported to contain the data on his hard drive and instead gave Hazen CDs containing rap music. The trouble, however, is that Hazen did not deliver the CDs to Best Buy, nor did Hazen ever have possession of the CDs. Rather, Best Buy is alleged to have created the CDs. . . . [T]o the extent Plaintiff claims a bailment existed with respect to the CD's he concedes he never possessed; such an argument would not establish a viable bailment claim. As Plaintiff plainly admits, he never received the CD's.

The creation of a bailment requires that possession and control over the subject property pass completely from the bailor to the bailee. Given that Plaintiff never possessed the CD's; he could not have transferred possession and control of them to Best Buy. Thus, there is no cognizable bailment theory."

20.   **Answer (A) is the correct answer.** The treasure trove doctrine allows someone to gain title to old buried money that they find. The doctrine reverses the rule that things embedded in earth or attached to the real estate go to the landowner. Treasure trove favors the finder, even if the person is on the property for a particular purpose, such as constructing improvements, and even if the finder is a trespasser. As such, those who look for lost treasures receive the benefit of the treasure trove doctrine.

Answer (B) is incorrect because the treasure trove doctrine actually works against the landowner by awarding the items to the finder. **Answer (C) is incorrect** the treasure trove doctrine does not require the finder to look for the original owner of the property, for the age of the items creates a presumption that the original owner cannot be ascertained. **Answer (D) is incorrect** because answers (B) and (C) are incorrect.

21.   **Answer (C) is the correct answer.** In *O'Keeffe v. Snyder*, the court held that the discovery rule provides that the cause of action for the recovery of lost personal property does not accrue until the injured party discovered or reasonably could have discovered the facts supporting the cause of action. The Louisiana statute, by contrast, does not employ a discovery rule.

Answer (A) is incorrect because both the New Jersey court in *O'Keeffe v. Snyder* and the Louisiana statute allow possession of personal property to develop into ownership if the necessary conditions (the passage of 10 years in Louisiana and satisfaction of the discovery rule in New Jersey) are satisfied. **Answer (B) is incorrect** because neither state requires the possessor to have purchased the object in order to gain title. Instead, the possessor could have inherited, found, or otherwise acquired the object and later assert a right to title against the original owner. **Answer (D) is incorrect** because neither statute adopts a legal requirement of registry in a database of lost objects. Such registries are becoming more common, though, and other states are beginning to give their use legal significance in disputes about title to an object.

22.   Property law allows Laura to own a domesticated animal, such as a sheep. The fact that the sheep left Laura's property did not cause Laura to lose her title to the sheep. Elsa could assert some rights as the finder of the sheep, but those rights would fail against the claims of Laura as the true owner. The passage of only two days is far too short to give rise to a either an adverse possession claim or to a suggestion that Laura abandoned her sheep. By contrast, the Broens were aware that the sheep was not a wild animal, and instead belonged to Laura, and Elsa's claim fails against Laura's as the true owner. Remember, too, that the law allows the ownership of domesticated animals. If the sheep had been wild, then it would not be owned until it was captured (perhaps by Elsa in this instance).

23.   **Answer (A) is the correct answer.** The original owner of property that is later found by someone else remains the true owner and is entitled to get the property back, except when the owner abandons the property. Abandonment is demonstrated by an intent to surrender title to the property and an act consistent with that intent. Martha did just that when she used the stamp on the envelope to mail the ballot, with no expectation that she would ever

get the stamp back. The fact that she later realized the value of the stamp and then wanted it back doesn't defeat her initial decision to relinquish her ownership of it when she mailed the letter.

Answer (B) is incorrect because the stamp was not lost by Martha. **Answer (C) is incorrect** because the stamp was not mislaid by Martha. The stamp was neither lost nor mislaid because Martha did not accidentally part with her possession of the stamp. **Answer (D) is incorrect** for three possible reasons: it is not apparent that the stamp was old enough to qualify for the treasure trove rules, the stamp was not found buried in the ground, and it is uncertain whether a stamp would be eligible as a treasure trove, which usually applies to more durable items such as coins.

24. An engagement ring is one of the few types of property that results in a conditional gift. The state courts are divided regarding whether the condition is satisfied if one of the parties breaks off the engagement before the marriage occurs. But all courts agree that the gift is finalized once the marriage begins. Even though the ordinary rules for a legal are present (offer, acceptance, and delivery), the gift of an engagement is conditional on a later event (i.e., the marriage of the parties). Furthermore, a valid gift needs to be delivered, so Lisa's acceptance of the proposal occurred prior to the delivery of the gift. But the gift becomes final upon the marriage. I would not be entitled to get the ring back even if the marriage later ended.

25. **Answer (A) is the correct answer.** A valid inter vivos gift requires an offer, acceptance, and delivery. There is no evidence that Jose intended to give the money to Amy, so the requirement of an offer is lacking.

Answer (B) is incorrect because the money was in fact delivered to Amy, though that alone was insufficient to formalize the gift. Likewise, **Answer (C) is incorrect** because the gift is not formalized even though Amy accepted the money. **Answer (D) is incorrect** because Answers (B) and (C) are incorrect.

26. **Answer (D) is the correct answer.** Items that are embedded in the soil are real property, not personal property. The most obvious illustration of that rule is a meteor that crashed to earth millennia ago, but an ancient canoe that has become embedded in the land over the course of hundreds of years qualifies for the same rule. The landowner owns all of the land, so Ellie Mae holds title to the canoe as the owner of the land on which it was found.

Answer (A) is incorrect because the rules for finders — including the finder of lost items — do not apply to items that are embedded in the soil, which are instead governed by the law of real property. **Answer (B) is incorrect** because even that the canoe became real property, the owner of the land was Ellie Mae, not Wally. **Answer (C) is incorrect** because the canoe is treated as real property, not personal property.

27. **Answer (C) is the correct answer.** The owner of the currency depends on whether the currency is properly described as lost, mislaid, or abandoned. Plaintiff's best case depends on the claim that it should be treated as the owner of the premises for purposes of applying finders rules. The fact that plaintiff has the possessory right to the apartment in which the currency was found means that plaintiff should be the one responsible for keeping the mislaid currency in the event that the true owner later appears, just like a storekeeper usually gets to keep property that is mislaid on their premises.

Answer (A) is incorrect because the fact that the currency was so carefully placed in a box behind the cans on the shelf suggests that the currency was purposefully placed there by the original owner. That means that the currency would be mislaid, not lost. **Answer (B) is incorrect** because it is unlikely that someone would simply abandon that much money. **Answer (D) is incorrect** because the currency was never subject to a conveyance that would invoke the bona fide purchaser rule.

28.   **Answer (C) is the correct answer.** The bona fide purchaser doctrine operates as an exception to the general principle that you cannot sell what you do not own. One with voidable title can transfer good title to a good faith purchaser who does not know of the rights of others, but one with void title cannot transfer good title even to a bona fide purchaser. Void title is gained without a voluntary transfer, e.g., theft. Voidable title is gained by a voluntary, albeit fraudulent, transfer, e.g., payment by a bad check. Here, Crockett & Sons gained voidable title because Patricia voluntarily gave it the ring, and then Alexandra became a bona fide purchaser because she bought the ring from Crockett & Sons without any reason for thinking that the jeweler was not its true owner.

        Answer (A) is incorrect because the fact that Crockett & Sons acted contrary to its bailment will make the jeweler liable to Patricia, but it will not allow Patricia to get the ring back from Alexandra. **Answer (B) is incorrect** because Alexandra satisfied all of the requirements to become a bona fide purchaser: she purchased the ring from a party who held voidable title without any basis for questioning the veracity of the jeweler's title. **Answer (D) is incorrect** because Crockett & Sons obtained the ring with Patricia's consent and thus gained voidable title, rather than taking it without her approval, which would have given the jeweler void title.

29.   **Answer (B) is the correct answer.** The inscription on the locket suggests that it was a gift from the Senator to Lucretia. The fact that it was dated the year before and that it was found near where Lucretia had been further suggests that Lucretia had received the gift that the Senator had given to her, which completes the legal requirements for an effective gift. There is no evidence that Lucretia intended to voluntarily abandon the locket, so it remains her property.

        Answer (A) is incorrect because the inscription and its date suggest that the Senator gave the locket to Lucreta, so it became her property. **Answer (C) is incorrect** because Paula's claim as a finder fails against Lucretia, who is the true owner who never abandoned title to the locket. **Answer (D) is incorrect** because the inscription on the locket notified StuffMart that it was probably owned by Lucretia, and any bailment that the store initiated by inviting Paula to leave the locket for polishing did not give StuffMart title to the property against its true owner, Lucretia.

30.   **Answer (C) is the correct answer.** In *Moore v. Regents of the University of California*, the California Supreme Court considered the status of a line of cells that a hospital took from a patient during the course of medical treatment. The court held that one does not have a property right in removed body parts to support a claim to conversion, but removed body parts can only be used for other purposes if informed consent was obtained. The effect of that holding is that Gomez cannot bring a conversion claim against the student.

        Answer (A) is incorrect because *Moore* indicates that the stem cell line is not treated as property for purposes of a conversion action. **Answer (B) is incorrect** because the stem cell line may be treated as property for other purposes. If, for example, the student had stolen the stem cell line from Gomez and then tried to sell it himself, the student would likely be subject to prosecution for theft. **Answer (D) is incorrect** because while a conversion action may be allowed, a stem cell line may be treated as property for other purposes.

31. **Answer (D) is the correct answer.** Laura began with title to the doll. Her intended gift to Julia was never finalized because Julia did not accept it when Laura attempted to deliver it to her, and then Julia's later acceptance occurred without her actually accepting delivery. The doll thus remained Laura's property when they left for the restaurant. Laura's placement of the doll on the public bench is evidence that she mislaid the doll; the doll was not lost for purposes of property law because Laura intentionally put it on the bench. Ellen, the finder, gained title to the doll against everyone except Laura. That title was voidable, not void, because Ellen did not take the doll from Laura against her will. Margaret had no basis for questioning that title when the doll was offered for sale, so she gets to keep the doll as a bona fide purchaser.

    Answer (A) is incorrect because Laura's claim fails against Margaret's, who is a bona fide purchaser. **Answer (B) is incorrect** because Julia never accepted the gift from Laura, and even if she had, Julia would lose the doll to Margaret as a bona fide purchaser, too. **Answer (C) is incorrect** because Ellen sold the doll to Margaret, thus relinquishing Ellen's title.

32. **Answer (D) is the correct answer.** At the beginning of the question, Esther owned the watch that she inherited from her grandmother. Esther cannot be found now, so she is not one of the options for who has title to the watch in her absence. Esther's placement of the watch on the counter of the Dickens grocery store made the watch mislaid property, which is generally held by the premises pending any future claim by the true owner. Cara's claim as the finder will fail against the store because the watch was mislaid, not lost. Betsy then found the watch where Cara lost it, but at that point the store had a better claim than Cara, so the store has a better claim against Betsy, too. And, Andy cannot gain good title by stealing the watch. The Dickens grocery store, therefore, owns the watch as mislaid property.

    Answer (A) is incorrect because one cannot gain good title to property by stealing it. **Answer (B) is incorrect** because Betsy's claim as the finder of the lost watch is inferior to the claim of the party who owned it before her — the store. **Answer (C) is incorrect** because Cara's claim as the finder fails becaue the watch was mislaid, and thus owned by the Dickens grocery store as the owner of the premises.

33. **Answer (B) is the correct answer.** Aunt Sue's death was unexpected, so the gift causa mortis doctrine does not apply to her efforts to give the stock and the money from the checking account to her nieces. Instead, applying the rules for an inter vivos gift, the transfer of the stock to the nieces was successful: Aunt Sue intended to make the gift, the nieces accepted it, and the title to the stock was delivered before Aunt Sue died. But Aunt Sue failed to deliver the $1,000 cash for each niece before she died, so that attempted gift is ineffective.

    Answer (A) is incorrect because the gift of the stock was successful, but not the gift of the cash. **Answer (C) is incorrect** with respect to both items: the stock was successfully given to the nieces, but the cash was not. **Answer (D) is incorrect** because the gift of the stock was successful, but not the gift of the cash.

34.   **Answer (C) is the correct answer.** The Martins accepted a gratuitous bailment of the furniture because they took possession solely for Norma's benefit. Breach of a gratuitous bailment occurs only if there was gross negligence, willful acts, or fraud. There is no evidence that the Martins engaged in any willful acts or fraud with respect to Norma's furniture, and the fact that the leaky roof was just discovered suggests that Norma will not be able to establish gross negligence, either.

    Answer (A) is incorrect because Norma did not compensate the Martins in any way that would have made them a bailee for hire. **Answer (B) is incorrect** because a bailee is not strictly liable for any damage to the good in their possession. **Answer (D) is incorrect** because water damage could result in liability if it satisfied the gross negligence standard.

35.   **Answer (D) is the correct answer.** James's use of the car was permissive by the consent of his mother Ann, the car's true owner. James voluntarily gave the car to William, which gave William voidable title. William's subsequent sale made Helmkamp Motors a bona fide purchaser. There was nothing about the transaction that should have alerted Helmkamp Motors to the fact that William was not the true owner of the car, so Helmkamp Motors gets to keep the car as a bona fide purchaser.

    Answer (A) is incorrect because Ann's claim as the original true owner fails against Helmkamp Motors' claim as a bona fide purchaser. **Answer (B) is incorrect** because James voluntarily conveyed the car to William, even though James never had title to the car to begin with. **Answer (C) is incorrect** because William, too, voluntarily conveyed the car to Helmkamp Motors, even though William's claim would have failed against Ann.

36.   **Answer (B) is the correct answer.** The test for infringement of the Lanham Act is whether the different marks are likely to confuse consumers about the source of the products. Consumers are unlikely to believe that a parody such as the one pictured here is actually produced by the holder of the Louis Vitton trademark.

Answer (A) is incorrect because there is no general First Amendment right to engage in parodies that result in confusion for purposes of trademark law. **Answer (C) is incorrect** because the use of different colors may not be sufficient to avoid confusing consumers about the source of the trademark. **Answer (D) is incorrect** because American law protects trademarks that originate in other countries if they are now also used in the United States.

37.   **Answer (B) is the correct answer.** Under state law, a raccoon is a wild animal that an individual may not possess. The exception to that prohibition exists if the individual applies for and obtains a permit from the local animal control authorities. The Bilidas would have been able to keep their raccoon if they had obtained such a permit — but in this case they failed to do so.

Answer (A) is incorrect because the government is entitled to regulate the possession of raccoons without having to prove whether a particular raccoon has rabies or otherwise poses a threat to the community. **Answer (C) is incorrect** because the statutory designation of "companion animals" only applies to those animals that may be legally possessed. A raccoon, by contrast, may only be possessed with a permit. **Answer (D) is incorrect** because the law does not allow someone to simply transform any wild animal into an animal that they legally possess. A wild animal becomes property only if the law authorizes that change, and a permit is needed to do so.

38.   **Answer (D) is the correct answer.** One has the right to use one's body, including one's knee. The right to use is a fundamental aspect of property, and the right to use one's right knee can be viewed as a property right.

Answer (A) is incorrect because it is generally illegal to sell one's body parts. The exceptions to that rule do not include one's knee. **Answer (B) is incorrect** because destruction of one's body is generally illegal, too. **Answer (C) is incorrect** because while there is a right to give some of one's body parts to someone else, that right is strictly regulated, and it generally does not include the right to give away one's knee.

39.   According to the federal Visual Artists Rights Act (VARA), if Jackson is an artist of recognized stature, then the university is prohibited from destroying or allowing the destruction of the mosaic. The university's actions appear to satisfy that standard, and thus give rise to a VARA claim. None of the other possible sources of law give Jackson a claim against the university. There is no state common law of cultural property. Federal, state, and local statutes and international treaties are the only sources of cultural property legal

protection. Nor would the university's actions constitute a nuisance. A private nuisance is defined as a substantial interference with the use and enjoyment of someone's land, and the university's actions do not interfere with any other landowners. Also, there is no authority for the proposition that harm to artwork is the kind of injury that qualifies as an interference with a right held by the general public, as required by public nuisance law.

40.   **Answer (A) is the correct answer.** Most jurisdictions that have recognized a right of publicity have also held that it is a property right that may be inherited. But if a court disagreed with that conclusion, then Einstein's right of publicity would have terminated upon his death. Hebrew University's claim depends on the argument that it received Einstein's right of publicity through his will, which would fail if the right ended once Einstien died.

   Answer (B) is incorrect because most jurisdictions that have considered the question have held that the right of publicity is a type of property that is alienable. **Answer (C) is incorrect** because federal copyright law does not dictate the content of state right of publicity law, and there is no fair use exception to the state law right of publicity. **Answer (D) is incorrect** because even if New Jersey law did not recognize a right of publicity when Einstein died in 1955, courts have held that a jurisdiction that later recognizes a right of publicity may apply it to celebrities who died before the right was recognized.

41.   **Answer (A) is the correct answer.** According to the federal copyright act, a copyright is available for any "original works of authorship fixed in any tangible medium of expression, now known or later developed, from which they can be perceived, reproduced, or otherwise communicated, either directly or with the aid of a machine or device. Works of authorship include the following categories:

   (1) literary works;

   (2) musical works, including any accompanying words;

   (3) dramatic works, including any accompanying music;

   (4) pantomimes and choreographic works;

   (5) pictorial, graphic, and sculptural works;

   (6) motion pictures and other audiovisual works;

   (7) sound recordings; and

   (8) architectural works.

   A toy train does not fall within any of these categories.

   Answer (B) is incorrect because it has long been established that photographs are eligible for copyright protection. Similarly, **Answer (C) is incorrect** because an article is a "literary work" entitled to copyright protection. And **Answer (D) is incorrect** because a song is a "musical work" entitled to copyright protection.

42.   Trademark liability arises where a new mark is so similar to an existing, protected trademark that it is likely to cause confusion among consumers about the source of the product. The fact that the covers of the two cookbooks are so different makes it unlikely that consumers would confuse them, so Lapine's trademark suit would most likely fail.

43. **Answer (B) is the correct answer.** The right of publicity recognized by most states only applies to famous individuals. If few people know about Keller, then he will not be entitled to the protections of the right of publicity.

    Answer (A) is incorrect because there is no fair use doctrine applicable to the right of publicity. **Answer (C) is incorrect** because a difference in shoes is not a sufficient distinction to avoid the overall suggestion that EA is exploiting Keller's likeness. **Answer (D) is incorrect** because there is no First Amendment constitutional right to use someone else's likeness. If there was such a constitutional right, then state law rights of publicity would be unconstitutional.

44. **Answer (D) is the correct answer.** Most states protect the right of publicity of famous individuals. The fact that Susan's book became a best-seller will make her sufficiently famous for purposes of the right of publicity. That right encompasses the right to control the use of one's image.

    Answer (A) is incorrect because the Wisco "99" trademark became part of the public domain once the company went out of business and abandoned the mark in 1978. **Answer (B) is incorrect** because patent law does not prohibit the description of an invention.; it only prohibits the unlicensed making of that invention during the duration of the patent. Nor did the company have a trade secret right to the patent itself, which is publicly available. **Answer (C) is incorrect** because the reproduction of the table of contents may constitute fair use of Susan's book, though that is not certain because of Elisha's commercial intentions.

45. **Answer (C) is the correct answer.** Parodies are not likely to confuse consumers about the source of a product because consumers are unlikely to believe that the user of a mark would make fun of itself via a parody mark. The Lanham Act is violated only if there is such a likelihood of confusion, so most parodies do not violate the act.

    Answer (A) is incorrect because there is no general First Amendment right to parody, especially when it occurs in the context of commercial speech, which receives lesser First Amendment protection. **Answer (B) is incorrect** because the purpose of the Lanham Act is to prevent the use of confusing trademarks. **Answer (D) is incorrect** because the fact that a parody actually improves the consumer perception of the source of the protected mark does not exempt the parody from the Lanham Act's likelihood of confusion test.

46. **Answer (C) is the correct answer.** The property law of all states allows individuals to possess animals that qualify as pets. The list of possible pets includes all dogs, including a Labrador retriever dog. The fact that Rhode Island law refers to them as companions instead of pets does not affect the possessor rights of the Robinson family.

    Answer (A) is incorrect because golden eagles are protected by federal law, and they may not be possessed by any individuals. **Answer (B) is incorrect** because most states do not include deer as they type of animal that may be possessed by an individual. Instead, deer are wild animals, even if they have been domesticated in fact, unless the state offers a permit application which the individual has satisfied. **Answer (D) is incorrect** because local zoning law is empowered to exclude animals from a particular place.

47. **Answer (C) is the correct answer.** An invention may be patented only if it is not obvious. Even though Morton received a patent, the infirmary may raise the obviousness of the ether's effects as a defense in an infringement action.

Answer (A) is incorrect because one may challenge the validity of a patent after it has been granted. **Answer (B) is incorrect** because patent law is unconcerned with mere thoughts about a potential invention. Morton would only be eligible for a patent if he took steps to actually produce the invention. **Answer (D) is incorrect** because patent law is a creature of federal statute, not the common law.

48.   Copyright's fair use doctrine means that someone else can use a copyright work even without the consent of the author. The author, in other words, may not *exclude* the fair user from the copyrighted work. By contrast, the fair use doctrine only applies to the *use* of a protected work, so the author still gets to decide whether to *transfer* the work, though again anyone who obtains the right to use a copyrighted work does so subject to the fair use doctrine. Copyright law allows an author to *destroy* a work, and the fair use doctrine does not provide an exception to that right. And the copyright owner retains the right to use a work even if it is being used by someone else pursuant to the fair use doctrine. In such circumstances, both the author and the fair user are allowed to *use* the work.

49.   **Answer (A) is the correct answer.** Federal and state law generally prohibits the sale of the parts of one's body because of a variety of ethical and utilitarian concerns about the consequences of authorizing the commercialization of the human body. You cannot, for example, sell your left arm even if the money you could obtain would be more valuable than the continued use of your left arm.

        Answer (B) is incorrect because one has the right to manage one's own body. In fact, the government is limited to the extent it can infringe on that right. **Answer (C) is incorrect** because the right to exclude others from your body has been recognized as a fundamental right, including for certain constitutional purposes. **Answer (D) is incorrect** because an individual has the right to use one's body, with only modest legal restraint (such as prohibitions on prostitution).

50.   The test for determining the infringement of a trademark under the federal Lanham Act is whether consumers are likely to be confused about the source of a branded product. A mark that operates as a parody of another trademark is unlikely to confuse consumers because they will not believe that the owner of the trademark would engage in such self-parody. Therefore, the parody of a trademark is permissible to the extent that it is not likely to confuse consumers. By contrast, while the First Amendment may impose some constitutional limits on the statutory protection for trademarks, parodies used in the course of business fall within the First Amendment category of commercial speech that receives less protection than other forms of speech.

51. The language in the conveyance to the railroad is durational: it refers to the railroad owning the lot "so longs as" it is used in the desired manner. The conveyance also expressly states that the lot "shall revert" if it is not used for a passenger station. The conveyance is thus sufficiently clear to overcome the presumption of a fee simple subject to condition subsequent, and to create a fee simple determinable instead.

52. **Answer (A) is the correct answer.** A springing executory interest divests the transferor in the future. O retains the present possessory interest as a result of the conveyance, but O could lose that interest to A if A becomes a millionaire. The conveyance thus gives O a springing executory interest. Moreover, that interest is valid under the Rule against Perpetuities using A as the measuring life, for we will know upon A's death whether or not A became a millionaire.

     Answer (B) is incorrect because it creates a shifting executory interest, not a springing executory interest. The future interest is held by someone besides the transferor — in this instance, by X. **Answer (C) is incorrect** because this conveyance creates a life estate for C, and then alternative contingent remainders in X or Y. There is no executory interest because the contingent remainders follow the natural expiration of the preceding life estate, rather than cutting short a previous estate. **Answer (D) is incorrect** because while D does have a springing executory interest, that interest is invalid under the Rule against Perpetuities because it may vest or fail at any time in the future. In other words, we don't know when — or if — the Chicago Cubs will win the World Series again.

53. **Answer (D) is the correct answer.** Dr. Key's great-grandchildren received contingent remainders. They are remainders because they follow the natural expiration of the preceding estate, to wit, the life estates held by Dr. Key's grandchildren. They are contingent because they will not become vested unless and until each great-grandchild turns 21. Contingent remainders are subject to the Rule against Perpetuities, and these contingent remainders fail under that rule because there is no life in being at the time of Dr. Key's death that can be used as the measuring life to prove whether or not the contingent remainders will vest or fail within 21 years.

     Answer (A) is incorrect because the contingent remainders created by the conveyance are subject to the Rule against Perpetuities. **Answer (B) is incorrect** because we cannot know during the life of any of Dr. Key's children whether or not they will have children who will then have their own children who will turn 21. **Answer (C) is incorrect** because Dr. Key may have more grandchildren after he dies — in other words, his children may have more children — and we cannot know whether or not those new grandchildren will have children who will turn 21..

54. **Answer (B) is the correct answer.** The owner of the life estate owns the present possessor right to the property so long as she is alive. The life estate is terminated upon the death of

its owner. Therefore, the owner of the life estate cannot devise it to her children — or anyone else — in her will.

Answer (A) is incorrect because the owner of a life estate is allowed to convey that interest to anyone else. The conveyance creates a life estate per autre vie: a life estate that is measured by the life of the original owner of the life estate, not by the life of the person who acquired it. **Answer (C) is incorrect** because the owner of the life estate has the present possessory interest in the property and may use it in any way she pleases, except that the life estate owner may not commit waste. Erecting a permanent structure does not constitute waste. **Answer (D) is incorrect** because Answers (B) and (C) are incorrect.

55.   A shifting executory interest becomes possessory by divesting or cutting short some interest in another transferee. Kim's conveyance gave Ron the present possessory right to the lakefront property. That interest would end, though, if Ron ever filed for bankruptcy. As such, Ron holds an executory interest. It is a shifting executory interest, not a springing executory interest, because it shifts ownership to a third party (here, Eric) rather than returning ownership to Kim. The shifting exeuctory interest is valid under the Rule against Perpetuities using Ron as the measuring life, for we will know upon Ron's death whether or not he ever filed for bankruptcy.

56.   Albert's conveyance gave Benton County a shifting executory interest that would become possessory if Dr. DeJong no longer used the property to provide medical care. That executory interest is subject to the Rule against Perpetuties. It satisfies the Rule using Dr. DeJong as the measuring life, because we will know oncer Dr. DeJong dies whether or not he always used the property to provide medical care. Therefore, Benton County holds an executory interest in the land.

57.   **Answer (A) is the correct answer.** The conveyance "to Lisa for life" in fact gave her a life estate.

Answer (B) is incorrect because "the first grandson of Lisa to marry Laura" has a remainder (because it follows the natural expiration of the life estate) that is contingent (because it depends on that grandson marrying Laura). Andrew thus has a contingent remainder that will vest (if he marries Laura) or fail (if he doesn't marry Laura or if another of Lisa's grandsons marries Laura first). But that contingent remainder violates the Rule against Perpetuities: there is no measuring life that can show whether or not Lisa will have a grandchild who marries Laura within the required 21-year period. So Andrew does not have any interest in the pasture because of the application of the rule. **Answer (C) is incorrect** because a court is likely to simply strike the invalid clause that would have given a contingent remainder to Lisa's grandson, which would result in Julia holding the future interest as a reversion after Lisa's life estate. **Answer (D) is incorrect** because the future interest held by "the first grandson of Lisa to marry Laura" is a contingent remainder, not an executory interest, because that interest follows the natural expiration of the preceding estate rather than cutting short that estate.

58.   **Answer (C) is the correct answer.** The conveyance from O gives B the property in fee simple, but that is conditioned on the property being used for a hospital. The conveyance does not specify what happens if the property is not used as a hospital, and it employs conditional language instead of duration language, so it gives B a fee simple subject to a condition subsequent rather than a fee simple determinable.

Answer (A) is incorrect because the conveyance gives B a life estate and C a remainder. **Answer (B) is incorrect** because the future interest is held by a third party, so C owns a shifting executory interest. **Answer (D) is incorrect** because O retains the property unless and until B turns 21 before O dies, which results in O owner a fee simple subject to an executory limitation.

59.   **Answer (B) is the correct answer.** The conveyance gives A a life estate and a remainder to Susan. But Susan's interest will be cut short if she writes a best-selling novel, and it will then shift to Dave. Dave thus has a shifting executory interest. That interest is valid under the Rule against Perpetuities: Susan works as the measuring life because we will know by the time Susan dies whether or not she wrote a best-selling novel.

      Answer (A) is incorrect because the conveyance gives A a life estate with a remainder for Dave. **Answer (C) is incorrect** because while it gives Dave an executory interest, that interest is invalid under the Rule against Perpetuities. We will know within the lifetime of Susan's preschool students whether any of them wrote a novel, but we will not necessarily know within their lifetimes whether any of those novels make the "Book of the Century" list. **Answer (D) is incorrect** because the conveyance gives Dave a fee simple determinable, albeit one judged by how long Susan teaches.

60.   Thomas devised his property to his wife, but is conditioned on his wife not marrying again. Thomas's children gain the property if Thomas's widow remarries. Thomas's children can thus cut short the possessory right of Thomas's widow's, which gives them a shifting executory interest. That interest is subject to the Rule against Perpetuities, but it is valid under the Rule because we will know once Thomas's widow dies whether or not she married again. Thomas's children will not take possession of the property at the natural expiration of the preceding estate; they will only take possession if a certain condition — the remarriage of Thomas's widow — cuts short her interest in the property.

61.   Buntin's conveyance gave LHA a fee simple subject subsequent. LHA will retain its possessory interest unless LHA failed to pay the mandated $600. If LHA doesn't pay, then Buntin's heirs may get it back, but only if they exercise their right of entry. The conveyance contains conditional language, not the durational language that would support a fee simple determinable. Buntin's heirs thus have a right of entry.

62.   **Answer (B) is the correct answer.** A has a life estate, B has a vested remainder, and C has a shifting executory interest that could cut short B's possession of Greenacre. C's shifting executory interest violates the Rule because it is possible that dandelions could be seen on the property at any time far beyond any life in being at the time of the conveyance.

      Answer (A) is incorrect because A has a fee simple determinable and O retains a reversionary interest that is not subject to the Rule. **Answer (C) is incorrect** because D's contingent remainder satisfies the rule using C as a measuring life, for we will know once C dies whether C moved to North Carolina. **Answer (D) is incorrect because** D's contingent remainder satisfies the Rule using A as the measuring life because we will know once A dies whether or not she had a daughter.

63.   **Answer (B) is the correct answer.** Leanna' will did not become effective until she died in July 2013. At that time, Wynbrooke Plantation was thus devised to Sara pursuant to Leanna's will. Sara is unmarried, so she has the present possessory interest in Wynbrooke

Plantation.

Answer (A) is incorrect because Leanna devised her property to Sara, and Leanna, rather than dying without a will and allowing Leanna's heirs to inherit her property. **Answer (C) is incorrect** because Sara remains unmarried, so Anna only has a future interest in Wynbrooke Plantation. **Answer (D) is incorrect** because Jeff only acquired the property that Sara owend in 2012. Sara did not inherit Wynbrooke Plantation until Leanna died in 2013, so the plantation was not among the property that Sara conveyed to Jeff the year before.

64.   **Answer (B) is the correct answer.** Ruby's conveyance gave herself a life estate. It also gave a remainder to Kurt. That remainder was vested because Kurt is an identifiable person, and he would take possession upon the natural expiration of the preceding estate. When Kurt died, his heirs acquired all of his property, including his vested remainder in the 120-acre farm. So while Ruby owns a life estate, Kurt's sons have a vested remainder in the farm.

        Answer (A) is incorrect because Ruby conveyed the future interest in the property to Kurt. Once Ruby's present possessor life estate ends upon her death, then Ruby no longer has an interest in the property. **Answer (C) is incorrect** because the remainder held by Kurt's sons is vested, not contingent. **Answer (D) is incorrect** because Ruby retained a life interest in the farm that lasts until her death.

65.   **Answer (A) is the correct answer.** The original conveyance from the county gave the city a fee simple determinable. The conveyance expressly states that the property "shall revert" to the county if it is not used by the city for municipal purposes, adding that the county need not take any act for such a reversion to occur. Accordingly, once the city sold the lot to Jessie in 1993 so that he could use the land for other than "municipal purposes," the land automatically reverted to the county.

        Answer (B) is incorrect because the city sold the lot to Jessie in 1993. **Answer (C) is incorrect** because Jessie acquired the city's fee simple determinable, and that interest automatically ended when the property was no longer used for municipal purposes. **Answer (D) is incorrect** because the state's claim to the property by escheat fails given that the property reverted to the county.

66.   **Answer (C) is the correct answer.** Olivia's conveyance created a life estate for Julia, followed by a life estate for Laura. After Laura's life estate, the property would either go to Lisa or to John, depending on whether Lisa was living. A remainder follows a life estate, and the remainders following Laura's life estate are alternative contingent remainders.

        Answer (A) is incorrect because a remainder exists only when it follows the natural expiration of the preceding estate, whereas here Lisa's interest would become possessory only if Julia's estate is cut short. **Answer (B) is incorrect** because while Lisa has a remainder following Julia's life estate, that remainder is vested because Lisa is an identifiable person. **Answer (D) is incorrect** because Lisa's interest does not follow immediately upon Julia's life estate, so it is not a remainder.

67.   Linda's will gave Andrew a life estate, followed by a remainder for the "such of the grandchildren of Andrew who reach the age of 21." There is no condition on the duration on the life estate, so it is not subject to a condition subsequent. Whatever happens when the life estate ends does not affect the fact that the life estate will continue for its natural duration, as measured by Andrew's life. The contingent remainder held by "such of the grandchildren

of Andrew who reach the age of 21" is valid under the Rule against Perpetuities using Andrew's children as a measuring life; we will know within 21 years after the death of Andrew's children whether or not any of his grandchildren reached the age of 21.

68. **Answer (B) is the correct answer.** The conveyance "to Angela so long as" gave her the present possessory interest in the undeveloped land that could be dispossessed if the land is developed. The "so long as" language has a durational component, which means that the conveyance gave Angela a fee simple determinable.

Answer (A) is incorrect because Juan retains a future interest in the property, which deprives Angela of fee simple absolute title. **Answer (C) is incorrect** because the conveyance uses durational language, not the conditional language that would create a fee simple subject to condition subsequent. **Answer (D) is incorrect** because Angela's interest in the property is valid.

69. **Answer (A) is the correct answer.** The original conveyance gave Elaine a life estate. It did not say anything else, so the Mountain Realty Company kept the reversionary interest as the original grantor. Nothing else that happened after that affected the fact that Elaine's interest in the 10 acres terminated upon her death, and the possessory right returned to the Mountain Realty Company.

Answer (B) is incorrect because Randy only received the property that Elaine could devise, and Elaine could not devise her life estate to the 10 acres. **Answer (C) is incorrect** because Sara didn't actually acquire any interest in the 10 acres from Randy, for Randy never had an interest that he could convey to her. **Answer (D) is incorrect** because while the county acquired Elaine's life estate, it was a life estate per autre vie that ended when Elaine died.

70. **Answer (C) is the correct answer.** Lisa never conveyed any estate in the land to anyone else during her lifetime. The permission that she gave to the Providence Church operated as a license that Lisa or her successors could revoke whenever they desired. Lisa devised all of her property to Jenny, so Jenny became the rightful owner of the land upon Lisa's death.

Answer (A) is incorrect because the Providence Church never acquired an estate in the land. It only had a right to use the land pursuant to the license granted by Lisa. **Answer (B) is incorrect** because a person's heirs do not have a right to inherit if the deceased wrote a will that devised their property to someone else. **Answer (D) is incorrect** because Andrew does not have any right to the land.

71.   **Answer (D) is the correct answer.** The owner of a future interest that is not even vested is not entitled to ask a court to partition property. Accordingly, the owner of the contingent remainder must wait until her interest becomes possessory (if it ever does so), and only then may be co-owner petition to partition the property.

Answer (A) is incorrect because co-tenants are always allowed to petition the land. **Answer (B) is incorrect** because any co-tenant may ask that the land be partitioned. Partitions in kind are preferred to partitions by sale, but there is always a right to obtain a partition. **Answer (C) is incorrect** because the right to seek a partition does not depend on the party owning a particular share of the land.

72.   When Herman died in 1931, that made Jerry a tenant in common owning half of the property, while Margaret, Julia, May, and Jennie were tenants in common owning the other half of the property. Then the conveyance to Earl and back made Margaret, Julia, May, and Jennie joint tenants for that half of the property. Julia survived the other three parties, so she took their shares by the right of survivorship. When Julia died, she owned half of the property as a tenant in common, and Jerry's heirs inherited his half of the property as a tenant in common.

73.   **Answer (D) is the correct answer.** A tenancy by the entirety is a unique form of property ownership that is only available to married couples. The theory of a tenancy by the entirety is that a husband and wife own property as a single, collective entity — comprised of the spouses together — rather than owning it as two separate people.

Answer (A) is incorrect because neither the husband nor the wife own any of the property in their individual capacities. **Answer (B) is incorrect** because co-tenants involve multiple separate parties as owners, not the single entity that owns a tenancy by the entirety. **Answer (C) is incorrect** because a tenancy by the entirety does not involve any specific resolution if the married couple later gets divorced. Any property owned by the husband and wife as tenants by the entirety will be divided pursuant to the otherwise applicable rules governing property distribution on divorce.

74.   **Answer (D) is the correct answer.** Courts in divorce actions in community property states begin with the understanding that the married couple owns all of their property equally. Upon divorce, some states direct the property to be divided equally, while others require an equitable distribution. The earning capacity of each spouse is such an equitable factor that is more likely to be considered by courts than any of the other listed factors.

Answer (A) is incorrect because most jurisdictions follow a no-fault approach that refuses to consider each spouse's fidelity as a basis for dividing property upon divorce. **Answer (B) is incorrect** because whether the husband or wife holds legal title to property is irrelevant in a community property state. **Answer (C) is incorrect** because while some courts may consider each spouse's household responsibilities, courts are more likely to consider the earning capacity of each spouse when dividing their property in a divorce action.

75.   Keys's will expressly created a joint tenancy, not a tenancy in common. Rebeck's death in 2008 triggered the right of survivorship and made the Central Avenue United Methodist Church the sole owner of the property. When that church dissolved in 2009, that property was included in all of the property that was transferred to the United Methodist Church.

76.   **Answer (B) is the correct answer.** A spouse may be held liable for waste of marital assets in either a community property or a common law jurisdiction. Additionally, in a community property state, a spouse is limited with respect to use of the couple's assets in a manner that does not constitute waste, because of the theory that marriage is an economic partnership and each spouse has an equal interest in all of the couple's assets.

      Answer (A) is incorrect because a spouse may own separate title to an asset, though that title will be irrelevant if there is a divorce proceeding. **Answer (C) is incorrect** because while whether property is divided equally or equitably varies between jurisidctions, the variance between jurisdictions does not depend on whether it is a community or common law state. **Answer (D) is incorrect** because Answers (A) and (C) are incorrect.

77.   When Ben sold his interest to Jackson, that made Jackson a tenant in common for one-third of the property while Claire and Kevin remained joint tenants for the other two-thirds. Kevin's death ended his interest in the property because Claire obtained that one-third through the right of survivorship; so upon Kevin's death, Claire owned two-thirds of the property and Jackson owned one-thirds as tenants in common. Claire's sale to Becky simply substituted Becky for Claire as the tenant in common with Jackson.

78.   **Answer (A) is the correct answer.** Property division upon divorce in a community property state considers a variety of equitable factors, but some factors are more likely to be given weight than others. The length of the marriage is one of the most significant factors because it indicates how long the parties were involved in a partnership that resulted in the sharing of their economic assets.

      Answer (B) is incorrect because many states do not consider which party was at fault for ending the marriage, though some states may consider that factor. **Answer (C) is incorrect** because title to property is irrelevant to determining ownership in a community property state. **Answer (D) is incorrect** because **Answers (B) and (C) are incorrect.**

79.   The original conveyance from the bank is unclear. It expressly states that the parties are to own the property "as joint tenants, not as tenants in common." But it also states that their assigns and survivors will then take the property, which suggests that there is no right of survivorship and that the conveyance is instead for a tenancy in common. The courts today presume that an ambiguous conveyance creates a tenancy in common, so the original conveyance made Nathan and Alice tenants in common. Nathan then employed the same language in his conveyance to Frank and Roxa, which resulted in tenancy in common for them obtaining Nathan's one-half interest (or 1/4 interest each for Frank and Roxa), while Alice retained her one-half interest as a tenant in common. Nathan had already conveyed his entire interest in the property before he died, so the interests of the parties remained the same.

80. Trudy's 1975 conveyance gave Thomas the nine acres in fee simple absolute. (Historically, a conveyance "to A for life, then to A's heirs" created a fee tail, but all states have abolished that device.) Thomas then established a tenancy by the entirety with his wife Almedia. The tenancy by the entirety ended when Thomas died because only a married couple can own property in a tenancy by the entirety. And a tenancy in common results when a tenancy by the entirety ends, unless the parties specifically say otherwise. Therefore, Almedia and Steve inherited the interest from Thomas as tenants in common.

81. **Answer (B) is the correct answer.** In *United States v. Craft*, the Court held that property held as a tenancy by the entirety under Michigan state law was nonetheless the property of Mr. Craft for purposes of federal income tax law. Ordinarily, a tenancy by the entirety is owned by the husband and wife and a single entity, so neither the husband nor the wife own a distinct interest in the property. But the federal income tax law covers "right to property," not just "property." The Court thus employed the bundle of sticks metaphor to find that Mr. Craft's interest in the tenancy by the entirety gave him a "right to property" for purposes of the federal tax law.

     Answer (A) is incorrect because the Court actually departed from the way in which Michigan law defines a tenancy by the entirety as property owned by the husband and wife as a single entity. **Answer (C) is incorrect** because the Court did not consider the status of the tenancy by the entirety in any other state besides Michigan. More specifically, the Court's holding only examined that nature of a tenancy by the entirety as a "right to property" as that term is used in federal tax law. **Answer (D) is incorrect** because the biblical teaching that helped shape the development of the tenancy by the entirety was irrelevant to the Court's interpretation of federal tax law.

82. **Answer (A) is the correct answer.** William's will did not become effective until he died, which was two weeks after Lance died. So at the time of William's death, Lance and Paula acquired the farm as joint tenants. But Lance was already dead, so Paula obtained the interest to the entire farm through the right of survivorship.

     Answer (B) is incorrect because the property was held as a joint tenancy, so neither party's heirs can obtain the farm after the original joint tenant dies. **Answer (C) is incorrect** because the will specified that Lance owned the property as a joint tenant, not Lance's heirs. A party's heirs can never inherit property held in a joint tenancy. **Answer (D) is incorrect** because William devised his farm in his will, so his heirs do not have a claim to it.

83. **Answer (A) is the correct answer.** Jill's student loan debt predated her marriage, so it will not be regarded as part of the marital estate. Jill's liability for that debt will remain her obligation and will not be shared with Jack during a divorce proceeding.

     Answer (B) is incorrect because both Jack and Jill used the credit card during their marriage, so they will both be responsible for paying its balance. **Answer (C) is incorrect** because while Jill retains possession of the house, there is no indication that it belongs to her alone. Jack and Jill will both have to pay for the mortgage unless they specifically provide otherwise. **Answer (D) is incorrect** because Jack and Jill remain cotenants with an equal right to use the house. Jill would only have to pay rent if she sought to exclude Jack, or if the rent was part of a setoff from other costs associated with the house.

84. **Answer (B) is the correct answer.** Anita and Greg had an equal right to the pickup truck

while they were still married. Both parties, though, were under an obligation to commit waste, which is a a voluntary, injurious act that has more than a trivial effect. Anita's keying the car thus constitutes waste, so she will be liable to Greg for the damage that she caused.

Answer (A) is incorrect because Greg and Anita both bought the pickup truck. The fact that Greg was the one who drove it does not change Anita's property interest in the truck. **Answer (C) is incorrect** because the marital duty not to engage in waste exists regardless of formal title to the truck. **Answer (D) is incorrect** because Anita's property right to the truck did not include the right to destroy it. The right to property usually included the right to destroy, but not if the actions of one co-owner constitute waste.

85.   Sarah's interest in the land reverted to David when Sarah moved to North Carolina, thereby returning David and Sarah to their original position as tenants in common. Sarah was allowed to to the interest that David conveyed to her to Hall Realty, so Hall Realty now owns Sarah's interest in the property. David and Hall Realty are thus tenants in common.

86. Janice has been staying in the house with the consent of CT Realty. That agreement created a tenancy at will. The tenancy at will that was established by the implied conduct continues for an indefinite duration, but it may be terminated by either party upon notice. Therefore, Janice must leave when CT Realty asks her to go.

87. **Answer (A) is the correct answer.** A tenant such as Thelma is responsible for evicting trespassers once she actually takes possession. Francis was trespasser, so it was Thelma's duty to remove her, not Lance's. Thelma thus has no excuse for not paying the rent that she owed to Lance.

     Answer (B) is incorrect because Francis has not entered into a lease or any other agreement that obligates her to pay Lance (or, for that matter, Thelma) for the estate. **Answers (C) and (D) are incorrect** because there was no interference with Thelma's premises when Lance delivered them to her in 1995. Francis arrived five years later, so any duty to deliver the premises had long since been satisfied, regardless of whether the American or English rule for the delivery of possession applied.

88. **Answer (C) is the correct answer.** Rent control laws are consistent with federal and state constitutional provisions only if the laws guarantee landlords a reasonable amount of rents. While there is no bright-line test for the precise return to which a landlord is entitled, an ordinance limiting a landlord's rent increases to 50% of the annual inflation rate is undoubtedly the most constitutionally problematic of any of the ordinances listed here.

     Answer (A) is incorrect because rent control ordinances have been commonly upheld absent a war, notwithstanding the original emergency rationale for the constitutionality of rent controls. **Answer (B) is incorrect** because it simply describes the cash flow method of determining the return to which a landlord is entitled. The cash flow method is one of several methods that courts have upheld in judging the minimum return to which a landlord is entitled. **Answer (D) is incorrect** because rent control ordinances usually contain such succession provisions, and they have not only upheld them, but courts have extended them to broader understandings of "family members," too.

89. **Answer (D) is the correct answer.** In most jurisdictions, the implied warranty of habitability does not extend to commercial properties.

     Answer (A) is incorrect because most jurisdictions do not allow the implied warranty of habitability to be waived by the parties. **Answer (B) is incorrect** because the warranty governs the condition of the premises regardless of when a problem occurred. **Answer (C) is incorrect** because the warranty guarantees the condition of the premises, not just a landlord's effort to solve any problems. The warranty does not apply to problems that are de minimis, but that is unrelated to whether or not the landlord was able to remedy them.

90. **Answer (B) is the correct answer.** A periodic tenancy is a leasehold estate that lasts for a period of a specified duration and then continues for succeeding periods until either the landlord or the tenant gives notice of termination. As such, a landlord may terminate a periodic tenancy for any reason, or for no reason. That, at least, was the rule in Utah until the enactment of the Mobile Home Park Residency Act, which prohibited a landlord from terminating a lease without cause. A term of years, on the other hand, is a leasehold estate that lasts for a fixed period of time or for a period of time that can be calculated with a beginning and ending date. The automatic expiration of a term of years means that a landlord need not act to terminate the lease. Thus, **Answers (A) and (C) are incorrect,** while **Answer (D) is incorrect** because Answer (B) is correct.

91. **Answer (D) is the correct answer.** While the English rule implies a covenant for the landlord to put a tenant in actual possession of property that the tenant has leased, the American rule does not imply any such covenant or duty. The American rule posits that landlords and tenants are equally on notice that this could become a potential problem, and equally capable of resolving it. Moreover, tenants can protect themselves by requesting an express covenant if they are concerned that someone else may be occupying the premises. Under the American rule, then, a landlord does not have a duty to ensure that a trespasser like John Crosby is removed from the leased property, so D is correct.

On the other hand, the landlord does have a duty not to interfere with the tenant's possession, so **Answer (A) is incorrect.** The landlord's duty extends to someone who is there with the landlord's permission, so **Answer (B) is incorrect.** And the landlord has the duty to make sure that no one else claims title to the land, such as Bob Clauss, so **Answer (C) is incorrect.**

92. **Answer (A) is the correct answer.** A breach of an implied warranty of habitability is the most likely instance in which a tenant can leave her leased premises without having to pay further rent or otherwise honor the terms of the lease. While there are several alternative tests for determining what constitutes a breach, the basic premise of the warranty is that a landlord has a duty to ensure that the leased premises satisfy elementary standards of habitability. A failure to provide running water to an apartment for six weeks will satisfy that standard, so Linus will breach the warranty despite his efforts to remedy the problem.

Answer (B) is incorrect because a single, brief problem will not entitle a tenant to abandon the premises and avoid any further duties under the breach. **Answer (C) is incorrect** because it is doubtful that a landlord has a duty to Twyla to control the activity — even the crimes — of other tenants. **Answer (D) is incorrect** because few states have extended an implied warranty of habitability to commercial premises such as Tori's store.

93. **Answer (C) is the correct answer.** A sublease occurs when a tenant conveys part of his or her interest in the leased premises. When Julia rents the two acres to Franklin for seven of the nine years remaining on her lease, that constitutes a sublease.

Answer (A) is incorrect because it describes an assignment. Unlike a sublease, an assignment occurs when a tenant conveys all of his or her interest in the leased premises, as Julia has done in A. **Answer (B) is incorrect** because most jurisdictions will describe it as a partial assignment instead of as a sublease. A partial assignment occurs when a tenant conveys all of his or her interest in part of the leased premises. Julia's conveyance of one of her two acres, therefore, established a partial assignment. **Answer (D) is incorrect** both because it describes an assignment of less than the entire interest held by Julia.

94. A term of years ends automatically upon the expiration of the duration stated in the lease, so Susan will be able to leave without informing her landlord beforehand. Notice is required before either a periodic tenancy or a tenancy at will is terminated, so Susan would not be allowed to leave immediately without notice if she has either of those interests in the land.

95. An estate at will exists when a lease is for an unspecified period that lasts as long as both the landlord and the tenant desire. Only notice is required for termination of the estate. By contrast, none of the other leasehold estates characterize Rachel's lease. An estate of years lasts for a fixed time period or for a period of time that can be calculated with a beginning and an ending date. The estate ends upon the expiration of the specified term or the stated event or condition. A periodic estate lasts for a fixed period that continues for succeeding periods until either the landlord or the tenant gives notice of termination. An estate at sufferance arises when a tenant holds over after the termination of the estate. An estate at sufferance establishes a new estate that lasts for the period of the rent or as an estate at will.

96.   **Answer (A) is the correct answer.** A recording system provides all of the information about the title to the property. That includes the identity of the owner of the current possessory right, and also information regarding any future interests, liens, or other property claims. Easements will appear in the recording system, too.

    Answer (B) is incorrect because the relative priority of a claimant who has recorded their claim and a claimant who has not will depend on whether the jurisdiction has a race statute, a notice statute, or a race-notice statute. **Answer (C) is incorrect** because the recording system does not contain information about a property's defects. **Answer (D) is incorrect** because a recorded title is still vulnerable to a successful adverse possession claim.

97.   **Answer (C) is the correct answer.** The right to build a dock is one of the rights enjoyed by riparian owners. In the (mostly Eastern) states that follow riparian law to govern water rights, riparian rights attach to the owner of the land that adjoins the river or lake. The land owned by the Carlsons is not actually adjoining the water, so they do not possess any riparian rights. As such, the only way they can build the dock is if they get permission from the landowners who do possess such rights.

    Answer (A) is incorrect because the Carlsons do not have a property right to build a dock, regardless of whether or not it interferes with other users of the lake. **Answer (B) is incorrect** because the Carlsons do not have a property right to build a dock, regardless of need to cross anyone else's property to get to the dock. **Answer (D) is incorrect** because there is no indication that the Carlsons own any water rights awarded by a prior appropriation system, and prior appropriation law does not include the right to build a dock into a river.

98.   **Answer (A) is the correct answer.** A church, like other private property owners, has the right to exclude others from its property. If Lye seeks to enter the church's property without the church's permission, she will be trespassing.

    Answer (B) is incorrect because RLUIPA only applies to governmental land use regulations. **Answer (C) is incorrect** because there is no general right to cultural property absent a specific statute, and no such statute is identified here. **Answer (D) is incorrect** because zoning law does not regulate a private landowner's right to exclude.

99.   **Answer (D) is the correct answer.** Property that is conveyed "as is" does not come with any promises about its condition. The buyer thus assumes the risks of any problems, presumably because the buyer paid less money to acquire the property without any warranties. Duggan's purchase of the property "as is" means that he cannot later move to rescind the agreement because he was not aware that they were not ready for residential construction.

    Answer (A) is incorrect because Peacock Point had neither a contractual nor a property law duty to prepare the property for the purposes for which Duggan hoped to use the property. **Answer (B) is incorrect** because Duggan's lack of knowledge does not provide a justification for voiding the purchase agreement, especially since Duggan bought the property "as is." **Answer (C) is incorrect** because the reasonableness of the price does not determine whether the sale was valid.

100.   **Answer (A) is the correct answer.** The federal Clean Water Act (CWA) prohibits the filling or dredging of navigable waters without a permit. The fact that the Blue River has been used for international trade confirms that it qualifies as navigable water for purposes of the CWA. The city, therefore, will need to apply to the U.S. Army Corps of Engineers for a CWA permit before the city can engage in any dredging activity in the Blue River.

Answer (B) is incorrect because the rights of two conflicting riparian owners would need to be reconciled in court. There is no absolute right to prevent another riparian user from using the water in a manner that interferes with your own use of the water. **Answer (C) is incorrect** because while the sanctuary has the right to use the river, but that is not exclusive. Other riparian owners are allowed to use the river, too. **Answer (D) is incorrect** because the courts have never held that an impact on wildlife qualifies as a private nuisance

101.   **Answer (A) is the correct answer.** The federal Comprehensive Environmental Restoration, Cleanup and Liability Act (CERCLA) provides that the current owner of a facility from which there is a release of hazardous substances is liable for the cost of cleaning up those substances. CERCLA has an innocent landowner defense, but it will be unavailable to Frederica because she appears to have spread the wastes during the course of building the addition onto her house. An innocent landowner cannot have been involved in the release of the wastes, and a landowner who spreads wastes that were originally disposed by someone else is nonetheless liable.

Answer (B) is incorrect because CERCLA liability applies to the past owners of property only if hazardous wastes were disposed during their period of ownership. There is no indication that Julia disposed of the wastes here. **Answer (C) is incorrect** because Frederica cannot point to any warranty made by Julia about the condition of the property that would allow Frederica to void the sale of the property. **Answer (D) is incorrect** because there is no evidence that Julia misrepresented the condition to the property to Frederica. The fact that the orange substance was discovered only once Frederica began her remodeling project suggests that Julia may not have even known about the wastes.

102.   **Answer (A) is the correct answer.** The property law definition of a trespass is an unauthorized invasion of property by a tangible thing. Jim's golf ball is a tangible thing which crossed Tim's property — his property right to the area immediately above his land — without Tim's permission. Tim will thus succeed in his trespass claim, though the amount of damages may be modest.

Answer (B) is incorrect because Tim did not have the duty to warn Jim. Rather, Jim had the burden to obtain consent from Tim if he wanted to hit the golf ball over Tim's house. **Answer (C) is incorrect** because the fact that Jim hit the ball over Tim's property unintentionally does not preclude a trespass claim. Tim only had to have the intent to hit the golf ball; he did not also have to have the intent to hit it in a particular direction in order to satisfy the intent requirement of trespass law. **Answer (D) is incorrect** because a trespass claim can be based on a harm to property or even the loss of the right to exclude itself.

103. **Answer (B) is the correct answer.** The express terms of the easement give Oncor the right to prevent interference with its electric transmission lines. Fuqua's use of his land is limited to the extent that Fuqua must abide by the provisions of the easement. Therefore, Fuqua will not be able to continue his flights if they represent a hazard to Oncor's electric transmission lines.

Answer (A) is incorrect because the rights provided by an easement are not exclusive, so Fuqua could continue to use the burdened part of his land so long as he does not interfere with Oncor's easement rights. **Answer (C) is incorrect** because while precise application of the ad coelom doctrine to airspace remains unsettled, it is clear that a property owner has the right to exclude aircraft from operating at an altitude so low that it could strike electric lines. **Answer (D) is incorrect** because the timing of the construction of the airstrip and the transmission lines is irrelevant given the express rights that Oncor now holds pursuant to the easement.

104. Beginning in 1996, Ridgway used Plot No. 52 with the permission of the land's owner pursuant to the lease agreement between the parties. Ridgway has not done anything since then to indicate that he now claims to use the land as a matter of right. Ridgway's use is thus permissive, so his adverse possession claim will fail.

105. While the amount of time necessary to establish adverse possession varies from state-to-state, most states require about 10 years. No state requires as few as a year or two. Therefore, the Stantons have not used the property for the necessary duration to establish the required continuity.

106. **Answer (A) is the correct answer.** The restaurant "is using the easement to access only Yacht Club's property for a purpose to which the Club's property is properly put, that is, parking. Thus the benefit is solely to Yacht Club's property, notwithstanding the convenience the arrangement provides to patrons of" the restaurant. *Caribbean House, Inc. v. North Hudson Yacht Club*, 2013 N.J. Super LEXIS 190 (App. Div. Dec. 30, 2013).

     Answer (B) is incorrect because Caribbean House retained the right to exclude the restaurant's customers from using the easement even if it had allowed other parties to use the easement in the past. **Answer (C) is incorrect** because the right to exclude others may be alienated, and Caribbean House did in fact alienate that right when it granted the Yacht Club the easement. **Answer (C) is incorrect** because the general rule prohibiting the use of an easement for the benefit of property other than the dominant estate "has no application where the owner of the dominant estate is using the easement to access only the land to which the easement is appurtenant."

107. **Answer (D) is the correct answer.** The fire department's land is burdened by a covenant that runs with the land. None of the grounds for failing to enforce that covenant are present here, so the fire department's challenge to the enforcement of the covenant will fail.

     Answer (A) is incorrect because the presence of the liquor stores outside the subdivision does not undermine the enforceability of the covenant with the subdivision. The doctrine of changed conditions can render a covenant enforceable, but that doctrine requires a much higher showing of a change to the area than the mere presence of three liquor stores. **Answer (B) is incorrect** because a covenant remains enforceable even if it remains unpopular with a majority of the landowners who are bound by it, unless they move to use the formal processes for abolishing the covenant. **Answer (C) is incorrect** because the fire department's mere purchase of the property does not bar the landowners from enforcing the covenant if the fire department later wants to act contrary to that covenant. Laches would only apply once the fire department actually began selling alcoholic beverages and a sufficient period passed without any of the landowners objecting.

108. **Answer (C) is the correct answer.** Back in 1973, Herman reserved an easement to cross the eastern portion of the property in order to access the western portion of the property that he still owned. Nothing has happened after that which would terminate the easement. Therefore, the easement ran with the land which is now owned by the Wilsons, who must allow the owners of the western portion — the Hintzes — to use the strip to access their property.

     Answer (A) is incorrect because the express easement reserved by Herman did not limit the use of the easement to access for a specific purpose, and the current use of accessing the western portion of the property is precisely within the scope of the easement. **Answer (B) is incorrect** because the Wilsons cannot complain that the use of the easement interferes with the use and enjoyment of their land, because the Wilsons have agreed (by purchasing the land subject to the original easement) that the neighboring owner may cross their land. **Answer (D) is incorrect** because the zoning permission granted by the county did not take any property right from the Wilsons, so the Wilsons cannot make a successful takings claim.

109. **Answer (D) is the correct answer.** The new Restatement rule allows a landowner whose property is burdened by an easement to unilaterally relocate that easement to another part of their property if the party who benefits from the easement is not harmed by doing so. Most states, however, have yet to adopt the new rule.

      Answer (A) is incorrect because an easement may only be used for the purpose for which it was created. Any other use is outside the scope of the easement and thus prohibited. **Answer (B) is incorrect** because the owner of an easement is restricted to the use of the part of the burdened land that was identified in the original easement. **Answer (C) is incorrect** because there is no unilateral right to terminate an easement.

110. **Answer (B) is the correct answer.** According to the Restatement, an easement by necessity arises when "[a] conveyance that would otherwise deprive the land conveyed to the grantee, or land retained by the grantor, of rights necessary to reasonable enjoyment of the land implies the creation of a servitude granting or reserving such rights, unless the language or circumstances of the conveyance clearly indicate that the parties intended to deprive the property of those rights." In other words, besides the showing of necessity, the creation of an easement by necessity also requires that the previous owner of the land have used the burdened property in order to enjoy the benefitted property.

      Answer (A) is incorrect because the use of the property allegedly subject to the easement by its current owner is irrelevant to determining whether it was necessary to use the burdened land to enjoy the benefitted land at the time both parcels were owned by the same party. **Answer (C) is incorrect** because the necessity that may give rise to an easement by necessity must have existed when the property was owned by the same person, and before it was acquired by the party seeking to use the easement now. **Answer (D) is incorrect** because the use of the property by the current owner of the dominant tenement does not influence the claim of necessity that must be established at the time that the property was owned by one party.

111. **Answer (A) is the correct answer.** A private nuisance exists when a landowner suffers a substantial interference with the use and enjoyment of their land. The harms suffered by the residents of the subdivision could satisfy that standard, though that determination will be made by the trier of fact. Indeed, the court found a nuisance in *Sowers v. Forest Hills Subdivision*, 294 P.3d 427 (Nev. 2013), the case which gives rise to this question.

      Answer (B) is incorrect because shadows are not likely to be sufficiently tangible to support a trespass claim even in those jurisdictions that have been the most generous in allowing microscopic particles to support a trespass claim. **Answer (C) is incorrect** because there is nothing in federal law that preempts states from governing the location of wind towers and other renewable energy facilities. **Answer (D) is incorrect** because the fact that local zoning law permits an activity does not insulate that activity from a private nuisance claim.

112. An easement is deemed to be abandoned if it has not been used, and if the easement holder

has engaged in acts conclusively and unequivocally manifesting either a present intent to relinquish the easement, or a purpose inconsistent with its future existence. The Corbins thus abandoned their easement in 1992 when they planted the trees that make it impossible for them to use the easement.

113. **Answer (C) is the correct answer.** A conservation easement allows the owner of the burdened land to continue to use that land, except that the owner may not use the land in a manner that interferes with the conservation goals described in the easement. If the easement is designed to protect certain wildlife habitat, then the owner of the land may not use that land in a way that injures that habitat. The damming of a stream presents an obvious case of an action that would violate the conservation easement because the protected habitat depends on that stream.

Answer (A) is incorrect because most jurisdictions allow the conveyance of an easement in gross, which is how a conservation easement is best described. **Answer (B) is incorrect** because a conservation easement, like other easements, does not prevent the landowner from selling or otherwise conveying the burdened property. The easement will simply run with the land to the new owner. **Answer (D) is incorrect** because the conservation easement only restricts the use of the burdened land. Neighboring properties are not subject to any restriction, even if they share the same conservation values.

114. **Answer (B) is the correct answer.** In property law, vertical privity refers to the relationship between one of the covenanting parties and its successor and interest. Vertical privity is necessary in many jurisdictions for a covenant to be able to run with the land.

Answer (A) is incorrect because none of the categories of implied easements depend on whether or not vertical privity exists. **Answer (C) is incorrect** because an easement always runs with the land, regardless of privity or other factors. **Answer (D) is incorrect** because there are very few instances in which a covenant may be implied, and they do not depend on the concept of vertical privity.

115. **Answer (C) is the correct answer.** A conservation easement prohibits the owner of the burdened land from using it in a way that interferes with the stated conservation purposes. The easement obtained by the NHF expressly prohibits "development in a manner inconsistent with" the purposes of preserving the ecological values of the forests, wetlands, and watershed on the Thompson's land. That easement ran with the land, so Eighteen Enterprises must now comply with it. Eighteen Enterprises is allowed to use its land, including as a golf course, but only if it can do so in a way that does interfere with the environmental qualities identified in the conservation easement.

Answer (A) is incorrect because Eighteen Enterprises is allowed to use its land, even without NHF's permission. The conservation easement restricts some, but not all, of the uses of the land. **Answer (B) is incorrect** because obtaining a governmental permit is likely to be a necessary but not sufficient condition for building the golf course. Eighteen Enterprises must comply with the terms of the conservation easement even if it has received all necessary governmental permits. **Answer (D) is incorrect** because the conservation easement, like all easements, runs with the land and bind future owners of the burdened property.

116. **Answer (A) is the correct answer.** This case derives from *Voice of the Cornerstone Church*

Corp. v. Pizza Property Partners, 160 S.W.3d 657 (Tex. App. 2005). The criteria for judging whether a covenant runs with the land vary among jurisdictions, but they are all satisfied here. In particular, the requirement that a covenant must touch and concern the land is satisfied here because it relates to the use of the land: it requires that the land "be used for commercial/light industrial purposes only."

Answer (B) is incorrect because the mere fact that a covenant prohibits a certain use does not also make that use illegal under local zoning law. **Answer (C) is incorrect** because RLUIPA — the Religious Land Use and Institutionalized Persons Act — does not give churches a right to use their land in any way that they want. RLUIPA applies only to governmental land use restrictions, not to restrictions imposed by a covenant that was voluntarily accepted by the parties. **Answer (D) is incorrect** because horizontal privity is only needed — if at all — for the enforcement of a real covenant for monetary damages.

117. **Answer (A) is the correct answer.** The National Registry of Historic Places is a list of historic places throughout the United States. There is no federal regulation of private actions with respect to buildings that are on the list. Any protection of the historic theater would depend on state or local law.

   Answer (B) is incorrect because the $1 children's movie affects the way that the property is used, and thus touches and concerns the land. **Answer (C) is incorrect** because the covenant expressly requires a plaque that commemorates the theater's history, not one that celebrates Sony. The covenant satisfies all of the requirements needed for it to run with the land. **Answer (D) is incorrect** because Answers (B) and (C) are incorrect.

118. **Answer (C) is the correct answer.** The Statute of Frauds requires that the conveyance of a permanent interest in land be in writing. None of the exceptions to the Statute apply here. In particular, the fact that Brumlow acted in reliance on Beaver's misrepresentation may entitle Brumlow to recover damages from Beaver, but it will not result in the forced sale of the home site.

   Answer (A) is incorrect because waste only applies to two or more parties with a legal interest in the property, and Beaver never acquired such an interest here. **Answer (B) is incorrect** because the requirement for an easement by estoppel provide a right of use, but there is no analogous doctrine that applies to the transfer of title to real property. **Answer (D) is incorrect** because the fact that Brumlow has not actually begun to build her home is irrelevant to her ability to for Beaver to sell the land.

119. **Answer (D) is the correct answer.** BHI may have a valid nuisance claim because the county's road maintenance causes a substantial interference with the use and enjoyment of its land. BHI may have a valid trespass claim because the droplets are almost certainly sufficiently tangible particles to qualify for trespass liability even in jurisdictions that have a restrictive understanding of trespass law. And BHI may have a takings claim because the county is responsible for the salt that now physically occupies its property.

   Answers (A), (B), and (C) are incorrect because Answer (D) is also correct.

120. Springer's lawsuit will succeed. An easement by prior use (also known as an easement by implication) is implied if (a) the benefitted and burdened land were both owned by the same party, (b) the use occurred at time property was conveyed, (c) the use persisted for a sufficient time to show permanent, and (d) the use was "necessary for the proper and

reasonable enjoyment of the dominant tract" at the time of conveyance. Springer can satisfy all of those criteria based on Lester's use of the dirt road across the eastern parcel to reach the public highway. George thus received an easement by prior use when he obtained the eastern parcel from Lester, and that easement ran with the land to Springer.

121. **Answer (A) is the correct answer.** A private nuisance exists when there is a substantial interference with the use and enjoyment of one's land. Phyllis has satisfied that standard here. The harms that she has suffered — physical illness and inability to sleep — are commonly accepted as supporting a nuisance claim.

Answer (B) is incorrect because nuisance liability can occur whether or not the offending conduct is permitted or prohibited by local zoning law. **Answer (C) is incorrect** because the harms suffered by Phyllis are often the basis for nuisance liability. **Answer (D) is incorrect** because the balancing of the benefit and the harm of the activity is typically reserved to the determination of the appropriate remedy for a nuisance.

122. **Answer (C) is the correct answer.** Generally, a covenant cannot be implied. The sole exception to that rule occurs with respect to a reciprocal negative easement, which allows a covenant to be enforced against a property owner in a subdivision if a large majority of the lots in that subdivision have such a covenant, even though the lot to be bound does not. But the courts require a greater showing of uniformity within a subdivision than 50%, so the fact that half of his neighbors have covenants that would permit the construction of a swing set does not mean that he is bound by such an implied covenant, too.

Answer (A) is incorrect because a covenant that affects the structures that may be built on the land satisfies the touch and concern test. **Answer (B) is incorrect** because the courts have held that a homeowners' association stands in the shoes of the individual landowners within the association, and those landowners have the necessary privity. **Answer (D) is incorrect** because the enforcement of a covenant does not depend on a showing that the violation of the covenant causes harm in a particular instance.

123. **Answer (D) is the correct answer.** The scope of an easement depends on its stated purpose. The purpose of the easements on the land owned by the McConnells is for utilities and for access to utilities. The use of the easement for the golf course is thus beyond the scope of the easement. Moreover, the fact that the McConnells have objected to golf cart path and to the out-of-bounds markers defeats the prescriptive easement claim because the golf course has not used the land for the period of time necessary to achieve the prescriptive claim.

Answer (A) is incorrect the golf course's use is beyond the scope of the easement, and it has not occurred for a sufficient time to produce a prescriptive easement. **Answer (B) is incorrect** because the prescriptive easement claim fails. **Answer (C) is incorrect** because that prescriptive easement claim fails, too.

124. **Answer (A) is the correct answer.** Johnson's agreement not to allow any houses to be built that would block the restaurant's view of the lake was part of a conveyance with the restaurant, it touches and concerns the land, and it was intendeto apply to the houses on the land, whether or not Johnson still owned that land. As such, the agreement constitutes a covenant that runs with the land and which allows the restaurant to obtain equitable relief against Milne.

Answer (B) is incorrect because the restaurant seeks equitable relief, whereas a real covenant only provides monetary damages. **Answer (C) is incorrect** because the covenant satisfies all of the requirements for it to run with the land. **Answer (D) is incorrect** because the covenant's express terms prohibit houses that "interfere with the restaurant's view of the lake," and that prohibition clearly applies to Milne's house.

125.   **Answer (B) is the correct answer.** Both an easement by necessity and an easement by implication depend on the fact that both the burdened and the benefitted property used to be owned by the same person. Bardin will also have to show the requisite prior usage of the burdened land and the necessity for using it at that way when it was owned by the original party, but the fact that Merrill Lynch was the prior owner of both the burdened and benefitted land is essential to both implied easement claims.

   Answer (A) is incorrect because both implied easements require that the land have been used as now proposed by Bardin when it was originally owned by Merrill Lynch. **Answer (C) is incorrect** because the mere fact of continued usage, for any period of time, will not yield an easement by necessity or an easement by prior usage if the land had not once been owned by the same party. **Answer (D) is incorrect** because Bardin's claimed right to use the land does not depend on whether or not the railway formally abandons its rail line.

126.   **Answer (A) is the correct answer.** An easement may only be used for the purposes for which it was created. The easement here allows usage "for farm land, but for no other purposes." Hunting and ATV riding are not usage for farm land, so they are outside the scope of the easement.

   Answer (B) is incorrect easements run with the land and are not terminated by the death of the original owner of the benefitted (or burdened) land. **Answer (C) is incorrect** because the test for the scope of an easement considers the intended use, not the relative benefit or harmfulness of the desired use. **Answer (D) is incorrect** because there is no right to unilaterally change the scope of an easement. Some jurisdictions allow the benefitted party to unilaterally change the precise location of an easement, but none allow a change to the activities that are allowed on the easement.

127.   **Answer (A) is the correct answer.** While most easements give the holder the right to use someone else's property, a negative easement creates a right to prevent someone from using their property in a particular way. A conservation easement operates in that fashion by limiting the use of one's property to activities that do not interfere with the conservation purposes. A conservation easement is thus a form of negative easement.

   Answers (B), (C), and (D) are all incorrect because they each refer to a right to use someone else's property. A conservation easement does not provide an affirmative right to actually use someone else's property.

128.   Colburn reserved an easement that allowed him to continue to use the three acres that he sold to the railroad. That easement ran both with the burdened land (now owned by Philip) and with the benefitted land (now owned by Burton). Burton, therefore, now owns the easement rights that Colburn originally reserved. The scope of the easement is not limited to grading or repairing the railroad's tracks. Colburn reserved the easement simply "to use the land for my own benefit."

129.   **Answer (C) is the correct answer.** The reciprocal easements gave each owner a property

right to use the other owner's land. The fact that one of the easements is no longer effective does not operate to terminate the other easement. Instead, the easement will last unless and until one of the legally recognized bases for terminating an easement exists. The fence interferes with the Sluyters' ability to use the driveway, so it violates the easement.

Answer (A) is incorrect because the Hales are not allowed to do anything that makes it impossible for the Sluyters to use their easement. **Answer (B) is incorrect** because the possibility of accessing land in a different manner does not operate to terminate an easement that already exists. **Answer (D) is incorrect** because the touch-and-concern requirement applies to covenants, not to easements.

130.   Townsend did not claim a legal right to use the property until he brought the lawsuit. His use is thus presumptively permissive, so Nickell can revoke that permission at any time. Townsend has not done anything to indicate that he believed that he had a *right* to use the parcel. Installing the septic tank could have suggested that Townsend believed that he had such a right, but his persistence in offering to pay Nickell suggests that Townsend instead believed that Nickell owned the right to the property.

131.   **Answer (B) is the correct answer.** The purpose of the touch-and-concern requirement is to demonstrate that a covenant is related to the land and should thus run with the land, rather than being a mere promise between the covenanting parties that does not bind their successors to title to the land. Driessen's testimony about how the covenant affected the value of her property is thus designed to satisfy the touch-and-concern requirement.

Answer (A) is incorrect because the evidence of value of the covenant does not necessarily show that the parties intended it to run with the land. **Answer (C) is incorrect** because Driessen's testimony is unrelated to the relationship between the covenanting parties that determines horizontal privity. **Answer (D) is incorrect** because the testimony is also irrelevant to the relationship between the original covenanting parties and the successive owners of the land that determines vertical privity.

132.   The easement gave Scott a right to cross the company's land, and that right would run with the land to whomever acquired the property after Scott. But the company interfered with that right by building the communications tower, which blocked Scott's use of the road. The fact that the tower remained for 36 years operates to destroy Scott's easement because it represents a prescriptive claim to use the land notwithstanding the easement.

133.   **Answer (C) is the correct answer.** The courts give broad discretion to homeowner's associations to adopt and enforce covenants. There is precedent for not enforcing such covenants to the extent that they affect activities that occur inside the privacy of one's home, but the fact that children were able to watch Lance while he was on his porch likely makes the covenant enforceable.

Answer (A) is incorrect because the covenant is a private agreement that does not result in state action necessary to invoke the first amendment. The only context in which the Supreme Court has found such state action in the context of a private covenant was in *Shelley v. Kraemer*, which has understood to only apply to racially-restrictive covenants. **Answer (B) is incorrect** because there is no state action, and because it is unclear how the covenant treats a protected class differently even if there was state action. **Answer (D) is incorrect** because nuisance law does not regulate the possession of pornography.

134. Most jurisdictions hold that an easement by estoppel exists only if the landowner makes a misrepresentation that is relied on to the detriment of the party who wants to use the land. Both criteria exist here. Helga misrepresented her intention to allow the convention to use her land, while Oscar and the convention participants spent $100,00 in reliance on Helga's agreement.

135. **Answer (D) is the correct answer.** Sally may not have realized it, but her approval of the deed bound her to the covenants that it contained. The no flower covenant is related to the property, so it satisfies the touch-and-concern test as well. The only constraint that the courts have imposed on the enforcement of covenants by homeowner's associations is that the covenant must be reasonable. The no flower covenant may not make sense to Sally, but it is very doubtful that a court would hold that the covenant is unreasonable.

Answer (A) is incorrect because Sally's approval of the deed constitutes acceptance of its terms, whether or not she actually read them. **Answer (B) is incorrect** because the homeowner's association obtained its authority from the voluntary agreement of the residents, including Sally. **Answer (C) is incorrect** because horizontal privity is not one of the factors that must be established to obtain equitable enforcement of a covenant.

136.   **Answer (B) is the correct answer.** As their name implies, growth controls are intended to limit the overall growth of a community. Growth controls are indifferent about how land is used within the community, so long as the overall size of the community development is restricted. Growth controls, then, do not regulate which areas may be used for residential purposes and which areas may be used for industrial purposes (or for any other purposes, for that matter).

   Answer (A) is incorrect because growth controls do seek to preserve the existing character of a community, especially if a community is concerned that a rapid or sustained increase in its size will change the social dynamics of the community. **Answer (C) is incorrect** because traffic, pollution, and the other consequences of an increasing population are precisely what growth controls seek to limit. **Answer (D) is incorrect** because growth controls are often employed to restrain the burdens of providing more public services — such as road and sewers and schools — for an increased population.

137.   **Answer (C) is the correct answer.** Variances empower a local zoning board to allow a use when strict enforcement of the zoning ordinance would cause unnecessary hardship because of the unique nature of the applicant's property. Variances are authorized because the failure to treat such unique property differently could result in the zoning ordinance being held unconstitutional as applied. Scala's best argument, therefore, is that she will be unable to use her property unless she receives a variance.

   Answer (A) is incorrect because the village of Shoreland is authorized to try to preserve the tidal marsh from development even if other forces such as climate change are threatening it as well. **Answer (B) is incorrect** because Scala's proposed cottage would constitute a new use of the property, and thus would not qualify as a nonconforming use. **Answer (D) is incorrect** because a landowner must comply with all legal requirements in the zoning law (as well as other laws).

138.   **Answer (C) is the correct answer.** Generally, a zoning authority may decide which properties should be subject to different requirements. Rezoning of property is generally permitted, too. The only constraint on such zoning decisions is that the government must have a legitimate reason for the decisions that it makes. The desire for more consistency in the height of the buildings along King Street is such a legitimate reason.

   Answer (A) is incorrect because there is no general supermajority requirement for zoning changes. Some jurisdictions impose such a requirement, but there is no evidence in the question that Charleston is one of them. **Answer (B) is incorrect** because the National Historic Preservation Act does not impose any regulatory limitations on local zoning decisions. **Answer (D) is incorrect** because the ad coelom doctrine has limited force in modern property law, and the doctrine has never been applied to restrict the authority of local zoning law to impose height restrictions on buildings in a community.

139.   **Answer (B) is the correct answer.** The county government possessed the power of eminent domain to acquire land from private parties for a public use. The county will be able to pay just compensation to obtain the land from the Nature Conservancy, even if the Nature Conservancy would much prefer to keep the land.

   Answer (A) is incorrect because an easement by necessity requires both the burden and benefited land have been owned by the same party at the time the necessity to use the burdened land arose. There is no indication of such a prior single owner here. **Answer (C) is incorrect** because it is doubtful that there is a riparian right to build a bridge from one's land to someone else's land. Even if there is such a right, the county will not be able to realize its plans because the south part of the island would still be owned by the federal government and managed pursuant to the strict terms of the Wilderness Act, which prohibits motor vehicles and commercial enterprises. **Answer (D) is incorrect** because the National Park Service lacks the power to change which areas are subject to the Wilderness Act. Only Congress can designate — or undesignate — wilderness areas.

140.   **Answer (A) is the correct answer.** The City of Downey's ordinance is similar to historic preservation ordinances that have been enacted by other local governments throughout the United States. The courts have long confirmed that the state police power encompasses laws designed to further historic preservation.

   Answer (B) is incorrect because the city is not actually taking the property. Instead, the city is regulating the activities of a private party. **Answer (C) is incorrect** because there is no total taking of the value of the property within the meaning of *Lucas*. McDonald's can still use its land, and the fact that it cannot do so as profitably as it would like does not mean that the city's action is a regulatory taking. **Answer (D) is incorrect** because there are no federal historic preservation laws or other federal laws that would prevent the city from regulating to protect its history in this way.

141.   **Answer (B) is the correct answer.** Historic preservation laws are intended to *preserve* historical buildings, landmarks, and sites. Sometimes those historic places are threatened by natural forces; sometimes they are threatened by human development plans. The laws thus limit a landowner's right to destroy the historic features of the property.

   Answer (A) is incorrect because the owner of property subject to a historic preservation law may sell or otherwise convey the property to someone else, though the new owner will then be subject to the historic preservation restrictions, too. **Answer (C) is incorrect** because historic preservation laws allow the private landowner to exclude others from the property, even if tourists would like to visit the historic site. The government would have to use the eminent domain power if it wanted to open the property to the public. **Answer (D) is incorrect** because a private landowner retains the right to possess land even once it has been designated as historic.

142.   **Answer (C) is the correct answer.** Public accommodations laws prohibit businesses and other covered properties that are open to the public from discriminating on the basis of race, sex, religion, and other characteristics. If a business invites the public onto its property, that business cannot exclude people based on those protected characteristics. The laws thus operate as an exception to a property owner's ordinary right to exclude.

   Answer (A) is incorrect because trespass law seeks to vindicate a property owner's right to exclude, and punitive damages are an especially powerful tool to ensure that the right to exclude is protected. **Answer (B) is incorrect** because growth controls do not limit a property owner's ability to decide who may (or may not) enter their property. Growth controls attempt to limit the number of people in a community as a whole, but they do not compromise an individual landowner's power to exclude whomever they want. **Answer (D) is incorrect** because the Religions Land Use and Institutionalized Persons Act (RLUIPA) operates to restrict governmental entities that affect the ability of religious organizations to use their land consistent with the religious obligations. Those religious organizations retain the power to exclude people from their own property.

143. **Answer (B) is the correct answer.** Spot zoning is the treatment of an island of land differently than adjacent properties. Spot zoning is thus inconsistent with the overall aspiration of zoning law to establish entire zones of consistent uses of the land. But not all specialized treatment of an individualized parcel of land constitutes spot zoning. Many courts have held that the failure of an isolated zoning change to conform to the city's comprehensive plan is one of the best indicia of prohibited spot zoning.

Answer (A) is incorrect because there is no requirement that a landowner who wants to use her land in a way now prohibited by the zoning law seek a variance before requesting rezoning of her land, or vice versa. **Answer (C) is incorrect** there is no general requirement that a zoning board approve a zoning change by a supermajority, even though some jurisdictions do impose such a requirement. **Answer (D) is incorrect** nearly any zoning decision will benefit some parties more than others, and no court has ever relied on that justification when evaluating the legality of a zoning change.

144. **Answer (D) is the correct answer.** The law governing national parks throughout the United States contains a general prohibition on snowmobiling in national parks. Congress has enacted numerous exceptions to that rule, however, including authorization for snowmobiles in Yellowstone National Park. Only Congress may change the law to allow snowmobiles in national parks where they are not already permitted.

Answer (A) is incorrect because the National Park Service (NPS) does not have the legal authority to allow snowmobiles in national parks, even if the NPS finds that snowmobiles are consistent with the Organic Act's mandate to promote both the enjoyment and the preservation of national parks. **Answer (B) is incorrect** because not all snowmobiling will "harm" endangered species within the meaning of the federal Endangered Species Act. **Answer (C) is incorrect** because while the Wilderness Act prohibits the use of motorized vehicles in designated wilderness areas, snowmobiling is prohibited in national parks even in areas that are not designated as wilderness areas (unless, of course, Congress has specifically authorized snowmobiles there).

145. **Answer (C) is the correct answer.** The parish's ordinance is supported by the broad authorization of the state police power. Concern about insects and about fire is perfectly consistent with the goals that the parish is allowed to pursue under the police power. Given that the ordinance is valid, the Audubon Society's only argument is that the ordinance does not apply because its preserve does not contain any obnoxious weeds or other deleterious or unhealthful growths.

Answer (A) is incorrect because most jurisdictions allow local governments to regulate for the purpose of aesthetics. Moreover, it appears that this ordinance is aimed at public health, not aesthetics, so the Audubon Society's complaint would fail. **Answer (B) is incorrect** because the preserve would still retain great value, and thus would not result in a total taking of the Audubon Society's property under *Lucas*. **Answer (D) is incorrect** because the Wilderness Act only applies to federal lands. The Wilderness Act does not in any way limit the power of state and local governments to adopt their own legal protections for wilderness areas that they own or that are owned by private parties.

146. The gas station's use of its original lot predated the 1960 village zoning ordinance limiting the area to apartments only, so the gas station can continue that nonconforming use of its property. But the right to the nonconforming use applies only the land that the gas station had used before the enactment of the zoning law. There is no right to a nonconforming use on the remaining lot in the subdivision, so the zoning law prohibits the gas station from expanding there.

147. **Answer (A) is the correct answer.** The United States Forest Service is responsible for managing national forests pursuant to a number of statutes enacted by Congress. Many of those statutes call on the Forest Service to make scientific judgments or to decide how to accommodate multiple uses of the same national forest. Given this broad statutory mandate and the broad discretion to pursue it, federal courts routinely defer to the Forest Service's decisions.

     Answer (B) is incorrect because state courts do not extend such discretion to local zoning boards, in part because of concerns about the role of local political forces in zoning decisions. **Answer (C) is incorrect** because few divorce property adjudications raise questions requiring a high degree of technical expertise. **Answer (D) is incorrect** because the courts do not second-guess local government decisions to exercise the eminent domain power. The only role of the courts with respect to eminent domain is to ensure that there is a public use and to ensure that just compensation is paid.

148. The nonconforming use doctrine in zoning law allows a landowner to continue using their property in the same way that they had been doing before a new zoning restriction became effective. The company will not be able to rely on that doctrine, though, because its use of the land to collect and sort scrap metal began after the 2008 zoning law excluded commercial enterprises from the area. The zoning law thus prohibits the company from engaging in the collecting and sorting activities.

149. **Answer (D) is the correct answer.** The Wilderness Act does not impose any limitation on the number of people who use a wilderness area. Nor does the Act prohibit the use of animals to carry those people. Therefore, the high school reunion trip is perfectly consistent with the Act.

     Answer (A) is incorrect because the Wilderness Act prohibits commercial activities, even commercial activities as innocuous as a lemonade stand. **Answer (B) is incorrect** because the Wilderness Act prohibits the use of motorized vehicles in wilderness areas. The only exception to that prohibition is for motorized vehicles that are used to manage the wilderness area pursuant to the Act, which does not encompass driving tourists to see the area. **Answer (C) is incorrect** because several federal court decisions make it doubtful — though not certain — that the reconstruction of a historic building is allowed in a Wilderness Area.

150. **Answer (A) is the correct answer.** The National Historic Preservation Act does not impose

any regulatory restrictions on private landowners. The federal list of historic places compiled pursuant to the act is used achieve historic preservation by the use of other laws, especially state and local historic preservation ordinances. The act itself, though, cannot be used to regulate the activities of a neighboring landowner.

Answer (B) is incorrect because CERCLA — the federal Comprehensive Environmental Restoration, Cleanup and Liability Act — holds parties liable for the release of hazardous substances from their land. **Answer (C) is incorrect** because state private nuisance law is often applied to toxic waste spills that interfere with the use and enjoyment of neighboring property. **Answer (D) is incorrect** because the toxic wastes there have leaked across the property boundary and may thus be treated as a trespass.

151.   **Answer (D) is the correct answer.** Jim must establish undue hardship in order to receive a variance from the local zoning board. The mere fact that Jim wants to build a much larger home does not constitute undue hardship when he already has a house that he can live in on the property.

Answer (A) is incorrect because the new house would likely be a sufficiently distinct use of the property to prevent the application of the nonconforming use doctrine. **Answer (B) is incorrect** because Jim cannot establish that he has suffered the undue hardship necessary to qualify for a variance. **Answer (C) is incorrect** because the spot zoning rule only applies to changes to the actual zoning ordinance, not to its application to a particular property.

152.   **Answer (B) is the correct answer.** A public nuisance is an interference with a right common to the general public. Public nuisance law if often applied to the release of hazardous wastes that present a public health threat to the community. CERCLA operates to eliminate that threat by requiring the responsible parties to clean up the wastes.

Answer (A) is incorrect because private nuisance law requires that an individual suffer an interference with the use and enjoyment of their land that is distinct from the injury suffered by the general public. CERCLA applies more generally to the entire public, and its remedy is limited to eliminating the wastes rather than compensating for other harms. **Answer (C) is incorrect** because CERCLA applies even if hazardous wastes have not cross property boundaries. **Answer (D) is incorrect** because CERCLA contains a statutory list of parties who are deemed to be responsible for cleaning up hazardous wastes, and that list extends to parties who were not negligent within the meaning of tort law.

153.   **Answer (C) is the correct answer.** The ESA prohibits actions by private parties that "harms" an endangered species. Harm includes certain habitat modification that interferes with the breeding of the species. The fact that Carlos owns the land does not exempt him from the regulation of the ESA.

Answer (A) is incorrect because the ESA only protects a species if it has been formally listed as endangered or threatened. The ESA was not passed until 1973, and no species that have been believed to have been extinct since the nineteenth century are listed. **Answer (B) is incorrect** because the ESA does not protect endangered plants from private actions. **Answer (D) is incorrect** because the ESA includes a defense that allows the killing of a listed species in self-defense.

154.   **Answer (C) is the correct answer.** The federal Religious Land Use and Institutionalized Persons Act (RLUIPA) requires that religious organizations be treated the same as other

organizations with respect to governmental land use decisions. The stated concern about there being "enough of these people" provides strong circumstantial evidence in support of the Islamic Center's claim that the town has not treated it equally as required by RLUIPA. The Islamic Center may also be able to show that operating a soup kitchen is such a central part of its religious mission that RLUIPA's substantial burden test applies as well.

Answer (A) is incorrect because the police power authorizes the town to employ zoning law to establish its preferred vision of the use of land within the community. **Answer (B) is incorrect** because the courts have long recognized conditional use permits as an appropriate part of zoning. **Answer (D) is incorrect** because the Supreme Court has interpreted the free exercise clause to provide fewer protections than RLUIPA with respect to governmental land use decision.

155.   The best way to remedy the situation is to enact a new zoning law that undoes the special treatment for the mayor. It appears that the village council supports the mayor in his scheme, so a popular initiative campaign that bypasses the village council in order to change the zoning law is the best course of action. None of the possible lawsuits against the existing law are likely to succeed. For example, the mere presence of a shopping center does not constitute a nuisance. Even though the neighbors may not like it there, the harms that they suffer from the proximity of the shopping center are unlikely to be of the type or severity to support a nuisance claim. Also, the government has not engaged in a physical taking of any private property, nor has the government regulated private land use in a way that produces a taking under either *Lucas* or *Penn Central*.

156.   **Answer (D) is the correct answer** because neither of the challenges brought by Anna's Arts or by Betty's Beauties is likely to succeed.

Answer (A) is incorrect because Anna's Arts bought the land for its expanded gallery after the new zoning law was enacted, so Anna's Arts must comply with it. The nonconforming use doctrine does not allow a new use of property acquired *after* a zoning law takes effect. **Answer (B) is incorrect** because the switch from selling antique furniture to selling local paintings is not the continuation of the same use required to rely on the nonconforming use doctrine. **Answer (C) is incorrect** because both Answer (A) and Answer (B) are incorrect.

157.   RLUIPA requires that any governmental regulation of the land use of religious bodies must serve a compelling state interest and employ the least restrictive means of serving that interest. It is hard to imagine why a city would enact an ordinance prohibiting vertical grave markers, and it is almost certain that a city would not have a compelling state interest for doing so.

158.   **Answer (D) is the correct answer.** The National Historic Preservation Act does not impose any regulatory restrictions on the use of land containing historic sites. The act could limit the ability of federal agencies to fund or permit the new development, but it is possible that WalMart could complete its projects without needing any such federal assistance.

Answer (A) is incorrect because city zoning ordinances have been an effective tool in blocking the construction of unwanted big-box stores. **Answer (B) is incorrect** because growth controls laws could be employed to limit the size and number of new stores. **Answer (C) is incorrect** because Vermont could use its state historic preservation law to protect certain areas from development by WalMart or similar businesses.

159. **Answer (D) is the correct answer.** The federal Telecommunications Act makes it illegal for local zoning law to rely on concerns about the effects of electromagnetic waves as the basis for restricting the location of cell phone towers.

Answer (A) is incorrect because electromagnetic waves are not sufficiently tangible to be capable of causing a trespass, according to most state courts. **Answer (B) is incorrect** because the private nuisance claim will require proof of an actual harm to public health, not just unsubstantiated worries. **Answer (C) is incorrect** because such a zoning law would violate the federal Telecommunications Act.

160. In *Village of Euclid v. Ambler Realty Company*, the U.S. Supreme Court rejected a due process challenge to Euclid's local zoning law. The court added, however, that such laws would need to retain enough flexibility to avoid unduly harming landowners whose property is sufficiently different from the other areas in the same zone. Variances are the device employed by local governments to avoid a judicial holding that the application of a zoning law to a particular parcel of land violates due process.

161. Pasco County may impose the dedication requirement if it pays for the land that is dedicated. The county seeks to impose an exaction on the affected landowners. An exaction occurs when the government conditions the granting of a land use permit on the landowner's dedication of land use rights to the government. The U.S. Supreme Court has held that exactions constitute a taking of property requiring just compensation unless there is (1) an essential nexus between legitimate state interests and permit conditions and (2) a rough proportionality between the conditions and the projected impact of the proposed development. Pasco County's dedication requirement is likely to fail the rough proportionality requirement.

162. **Answer (B) is the correct answer.** The federal and state constitutions each limit the government's eminent domain power to acquisitions that qualify as a "public use." In *County of Wayne v. Hathcock*, the Michigan Supreme Court held that the public use requirement in the state constitution prohibits the government from taking property from one private party to give to another private party except in certain limited circumstances. The City of Austin's plan to take Block 38 and give it to the private developer is likely to fail to qualify as a public use under *Hathcock*.

Answer (A) is incorrect because the U.S. Supreme Court held in *Kelo v. City of New London* that the public use limitation in the U.S. Constitution allows the government to take property from one private party in order to give it to another private party, which would enable the City of Austin to acquire Block 38. **Answer (C) is incorrect** because no court has interpreted a public use requirement to depend on whether a property is only used for official government business. **Answer (D) is incorrect** because the purpose of the eminent domain power is to empower the government to force an unwilling private party to sell its land to the government for just compensation.

163. **Answer (A) is the correct answer.** Fair market value is the general test for judging the just compensation required by the Fifth Amendment. There are only a few exceptions to that rule. One of them applies if the fair market value of the property cannot be determined, which then requires that the court identify another method for determining what constitutes just compensation.

Answer (B) is incorrect because the courts deciding just compensation refuse to consider any family memories, the suitability of the land for a unique business, or any other special value of the property to its owner. **Answer (C) is incorrect** because the replacement cost is not considered in judging what compensation is just. **Answer (D) is incorrect** because the government's inability to pay is irrelevant to the determination of just compensation.

164. **Answer (C) is the correct answer.** The fair market value of the property will determine the just compensation that the government must pay. That fair market value is based on the legally permissible use of the land, whether or not that is the use to which the land is

currently put. The residential subdivisions allowed by the zoning law will be worth far more than Labak's current use of the property.

Answer (A) is incorrect because property acquired for a national park is a public use in the literal sense that the public is allowed to use the land once the government acquires it. **Answer (B) is incorrect** because the test for just compensation is fair market value. The fact that it may cost more to replace one's property does not usually factor into the calculation of just compensation. **Answer (D) is incorrect** because while Labak will be entitled to the value of the property for his current bird watching business, that value will be less than the value of the property for residential subdivisions.

165. **Answer (C) is the correct answer.** The fact that the properties still retain significant value means that there has not been a total taking. The *Penn Central* balancing test thus applies. The government did not actually prohibit the landowners from selling their land, and any reduced value associated with the failed negotiations will not suffice to establish a taking under *Penn Central.*

Answer (A) is incorrect the mere reduction in property's value does not constitute a taking, especially when the landowners have remained free to use or sell their properties. **Answer (B) is incorrect** because any future government taking of the property remains speculative and would be judged separately if it actually occurs in the future. **Answer (D) is incorrect** because the right to alienation is a central right protected by property law, even though that right was not actually taken by the government here.

166. **Answer (C) is the correct answer.** The vertical limit to property ownership occurs at the height designated by the Federal Aviation Administration (FAA) for navigable airspace. Air Pegasus has no right to operate in such airspace without the permission of the FAA, so the FAA's refusal to grant such permission does not deny Air Pegasus of any property right.

Answer (A) is incorrect because Air Pegasus still retains the right to use the property that it leased, albeit not for the purposes that it intended. **Answer (B) is incorrect** because the FAA has not physically seized any property right owned by Air Pegasus, given that Air Pegasus does not have a property right to navigable airspace. **Answer (D) is incorrect** because operating a heliport that complies with FAA requirements does not constitute a nuisance.

167. **Answer (D) is the correct answer.** Neither the total takings test nor the permanent physical invasion test applies to the government's failure to enforce the zoning regulations. The default takings test of *Penn Central* will thus be used to determine whether there is a taking.

Answer (A) is incorrect because the increased traffic does not constitute the government's physical invasion of the neighbors' property. The traffic does not even result in a permanent physical invasion of the neighbors' property. **Answer (B) is incorrect** because an exaction exists where the government conditions zoning approval on the landowner's dedication of land or money to the government, which did not occur here. **Answer (C) is incorrect** because while there is no taking when the government acts to abate a nuisance, it is doubtful that the noise and traffic associated with an expanded campus will qualify as a nuisance, and even less likely that the government will be held responsible for that outcome simply because it failed to enforce the zoning regulations.

168. The total taking test described in *Lucas* applies only if a government action has reduced a property's value by nearly one hundred percent. The fact that Peggy still has half of her customers means that there has not been a total taking. The courts have never held that a reduction of a property's value by fifty percent does not in itself demonstrate that there has been a taking. Nor would Peggy be able to establish a taking under *Penn Central* because the government is not obligated to ensure that her business remains profitable. It is also questionable whether a government decision to close a road can be a taking regardless of the economic harm that it causes.

169. **Answer (A) is the correct answer.** The U.S. Supreme Court had held that a permanent physical occupation of land is always a taking. That bright-line rule applies without resort to any balancing test. The amount of damages may be modest or even trivial, but the wells do constitute a taking.

    Answer (B) is incorrect because a prohibition on adding one room onto an existing building is not a total taking under *Lucas*, so it will be judged under the *Penn Central* balancing test. That test usually results in the finding that there is no taking, and the character of the government's historic preservation regulation suggests that a court would not find a taking. **Answer (C) is incorrect** because Julia will still be able to use her land for residential purposes, so it is not a total taking. Nor will there be a taking under the *Penn Central* test because of the justifications usually associated with the local zoning authority, especially if Julia has not demonstrated any investment-backed expectations to build a bed and breakfast there. **Answer (D) is incorrect** because the courts have repeatedly held that actions necessary to prevent a public emergency, such as destroying a house to prevent the spread of a fire, do not qualify as takings.

170. Leanna is entitled to the fair market value of the property rights that she owns. Her ownership right to the land is worth two million dollars because of the existence of the conservation easement. Leanna is not entitled to the value of what her property would be worth if it was not encumbered by the conservation easement.

171. Carrie should apply for a variance from the regulations. In many jurisdictions, Carrie will need to establish both that she suffers an undue hardship from the existing zoning regulation and that a variance will not be detrimental to the area. If Carrie can make that showing, then she will be entitled to a variance. Alternatively, Carrie could seek to have the zoning changed, which is a common procedure but subject to charges of illegal spot zoning if the change affected only Carrie's lot. Or Carrie could simply redesign her planned house.

172. The best legal authority for Lisa's claim that she is entitled to keep her "Bush for President" sign is *Shelley v. Kraemer*, 334 U.S. 1 (1948), because it establishes that a covenant cannot be enforced if it violates the Constitution. *Shelley* held that the invocation of the judicial process to enforce the private covenant constituted state action subject to the equal protection clause. If *Shelley* is extended to the first amendment, then the restriction of election signs could be unconstitutional for the same reason. The courts have been reluctant to extend *Shelley*, though, so the success of Lisa's case is doubtful. Another good authority for Lisa is *City of LaDue v. Gilleo*, 512 U.S. 43 (1994), which holds that a municipal zoning ordinance can violate the first amendment if it restricts political signs. But *City of Ladue* addressed government zoning, not private covenants, so it is doubtful that Lisa will prevail on that theory either.

173. The parking fee is probably invalid. *In Thanasoulis v. Winston Towers 200 Associates*, 542 A.2d 900 (N.J. 1988), the court considered a similar dispute. The court there acknowledged that a homeowner's association can establish reasonable parking regulations. But the court further held that an association cannot expropriate the economic value of an owner's parking space for its own use. An owner has the right to lease his or her unit, including the parking space and the interest in the common elements. Additionally, an association cannot discriminate against a nonresident owner assuming that the governing statute provides that an owner is only *proportionately liable* for his or her share of the common expenses. An association cannot require an owner to contribute three times more money to the common-expense fund for parking privileges than do other unit owners who do not rent their units.

174. This problem is based upon *Blockbuster Videos, Inc. v. City of Tempe*, 141 F.3d 1295 (9th Cir. 1998). Tempe cannot enforce its ordinance because it conflicts with the federally protected trademark owned by Blockbuster. Generally, a community can employ zoning laws to regulate aesthetics, either by dictating the desired appearance or forbidding an unwanted appearance. But zoning law is state and local law, and it will always be subject to the command of the supremacy clause that federal laws trump contrary state laws. The federal Lanham Act protects trademarks like the one held by Blockbuster. Tempe's effort to modify the colors of Blockbuster's sign will thus fail because such zoning would interfere with the superior federally protected trademark held by Blockbuster.

175. Charlie will probably not get the laptop. To be legally effective, Arthur's gift to Charlie

required both intent and delivery. Arthur intended to give the laptop to Charlie, but Arthur did not deliver the laptop to Charlie. Arthur appears to have decided after he took the bar exam to give the laptop to Charlie, and it further appears that the laptop had already been shipped. Nonetheless, delivery to Charlie never occurred, and nothing in these events would eliminate the delivery requirement. Charlie cannot get the gift as a gift causa mortis, either, because Arthur was not under an apprehension of death when he agreed to give the laptop to Charlie.

176.   One's vote for President is property within the meaning of the Restatement's understanding of "legal relations between persons with respect to a thing." A person has a right to use his or her vote, to not use that vote, and a right to possess that vote. By contrast, a person does not have a right to modify that vote, to sell their vote, or to transfer the vote to someone else even if no money exchanges hands.

177.   It does not appear that any court has had the occasion to apply other fundamental theories of property law to weather modification activities, but it is possible to imagine how those theories would apply. An occupation theory posits that property ownership occurs when something is captured and reduced to possession, so it would suggest that precipitation is not owned until someone captures it. An occupation theory might actually affirm the legitimacy of weather modification programs that "capture" precipitation before it reaches the earth. Likewise, a labor theory could approve such programs because it would honor the mix of a natural resource and the effort undertaken to improve it. A utilitarian theory would consider the reasonable expectations of the affected parties, which could support the claims of those seeking a natural level of precipitation, but which could also provoke a heated disagreement about the ability to modify the weather. It is more difficult to conceive of how economic theories of property might apply to weather modification programs, in part because of the variety of such theories, but general wealth maximization principles could support the use of weather modification programs if they help some landowners more than they harm others.

178.   The California Supreme Court's decision in *Moore v. Regents of the University of California*, 793 P.2d 479 (Cal. 1990), *cert. denied*, 499 U.S. 936 (1991), is the leading case involving the alleged conversion of a patient's body parts that were removed during the course of an operation and later used for medical research. The court explained that there was no conversion because a patient does not expect to retain possession of small body parts that are removed during an operation. Nor was there any precedent for such a conversion claim. The court also explained that a patient's interests were outweighed by the social benefit attending medical research, especially given a patient's admitted right to insist upon informed consent before any parts of his or her body are used in medical research.

179.   A tenant asking a court to recognize an implied warranty of habitability may advance a number of arguments. First, many courts have already found such a warranty, and those decisions provide persuasive precedents for a court considering the question now. Second, an implied warranty of habitability is more consistent with the realities of modern urban living than the older real property theories that denied such a warranty. Likewise, an implied warranty is consistent with contemporary contract principles that are informing the development of landlord/tenant law. Finally, judicial recognition of an implied warranty furthers the important public policy of assuring that everyone is able to live in adequate housing.

180.   The church is probably liable for a trespass. The ad coelum doctrine provides that the owner of land also owns the space above and the area below that land. The extension of the church's gutters over the store's land constituted a trespass. But the church will argue that it has adversely possessed the area occupied by the gutters. The church's gutters were there for long past the statutory period, and they were open and visible. It is unclear whether the gutters also achieved an exclusive claim to the airspace, though that seems likely. The hardest question is whether the gutters crossed the store's property under a claim of right. State courts are divided concerning the ability of an unintentional, mistaken location of a building to satisfy the claim of right requirement. Even if the church satisfied the claim of right requirement and thereby establish adverse possession, the store could still argue that the falling water constitutes a trespass even if the gutters do not. That claim is doubtful, though, for it is uncertain whether the redirection of natural rainfall is a trespass, especially if the gutters that work the redirection are there lawfully.

181.   **Answer (D) is the correct answer.** The issue in *Pierson v. Post* was whether pursuit or capture established title to the fox. But the fox was a wild animal before it was pursued or captured. Wild animals are not owned by anyone. The U.S. Supreme Court once suggested that wild animals belong to the state in which we live, but the Court has since clarified that the state does not have title to wild animals within the meaning of property law.

         Answers (A) and (B) are incorrect because neither Pierson nor Post had a legal claim to the fox before the fox was pursued and captured. **Answer (C) is incorrect** because wild animals are not regarded as real property that are included in the landowner's title.

182.   **Answer (B) is the correct answer.** Jack has a shifting executory interest that would dispossess Melissa of her estate if she no longer has a child or grandchild who practices medicine. Shifting executory interests are subject to the Rule against Perpetuities. Jack's shifting executory interest is invalid under the Rule because Melissa could have a grandchild who is not a life in being at the time of the conveyance or during Melissa's own lifetime, so there is no measuring life that can be used to validate the interest under the Rule.

         Answer (A) is incorrect because while Jack's contingent remainder is subject to the Rule against Perpetuities, we will know during his lifetime whether or not Jack ever opens a bed and breakfast, so Jack can be used as the measuring life to validate his contingent remainder. **Answer (C) is incorrect** because Jack has a contingent remainder that will only become possessory if Amanda graduates from college. We will know whether or not Amanda had graduated from college when she dies, so Amanda can serve as the measuring life under the Rule. **Answer (D) is incorrect** because we will know whether or not Jack's alternate contingent remainder will become possessory when Amanda or Gloria dies, so either Amanda or Gloria work as the measuring life under the Rule.

183.   **Answer (A) is the correct answer.** There is nothing in the conveyance which indicates that GMSB received anything less than the entire interest that Brewer had owned in the strip of land. The railroad may not have needed the fee simple absolute title, and instead may have been satisfied with an easement that allowed it to use the land, but Brewer's conveyance was not limited to a particular use of the land.

         Answers (B) and (C) are incorrect because GMSB's ownership is not conditioned on its use of the land for a particular purpose. **Answer (D) is incorrect** because the conveyance does not refer to a right to use the strip of land; it refers instead to Brewer's interest, which was in fee simple absolute.

184.   **Answer (C) is the correct answer.** The will, while ambiguous, obviously intended to convey some interest in the property to Dalton's wife. Dalton's children may or may not receive the property in the future, but the will cannot be interpreted to give them the current possessory interest, so they do not own the property in fee simple absolute.

Answer (A) is incorrect because the will can be interpreted to give "all real & personal property" to Dalton's wife, and the will's statement that Dalton wanted his wife "to share all of my property with my Children" may be read as a generalized statement of intent that did not alter the legal status of the estate. **Answer (B) is incorrect** because it is alternately possible to read the clause giving the property to Dalton's wife "till she dies" as giving her a life estate, with Dalton's children holding the remainder. **Answer (D) is incorrect** because it is possible, though not perhaps not as likely as the previous two readings, that a court could prioritize the will's desire for the property to be shared as establishing a tenancy in common between Dalton's wife and Dalton's children.

185.   **Answer (C) is the correct answer.** In *Georgia v. Randolph*, the U.S. Supreme Court held that one cotenant can not authorize a police search over the objection of a cotenant. McArthur voiced his objection to the search before it occurred, so the police were not authorized to rely on Wiles' consent to search McArthur's bedroom.

Answers (A) and (B) are incorrect because the formal legal status of the cotenancy does not determine the authority of one cotenant to authorize a search of their premises. **Answer (D) is incorrect** any cotenant can authorize a police search, provided that no other cotenant objects.

186.   **Answer (D) is the correct answer.** Both private nuisance and trespass law require affirmative proof that the offending nuisance or trespass has infact occurred. The mere possibility, or the risk, of a substantial interference with the use and enjoyment of the land or of harmful substances entering the property do not give rise to private nuisance or trespass liability, respectively. The plaintiff will only need to satisfy the civil law standard that the facts are more likely than not to exist, but Judge Wilkins concluded that the plaintiffs had not met that standard.

Answer (A) is incorrect because the plaintiffs did not prove that there was contamination that constitutes a nuisance. **Answer (B) is incorrect** because the plaintiffs did not prove that there was contamination that resulted in a trespass. **Answer (C) is incorrect** because the plaintiffs failed to provide the evidence needed to prove either of their claims.

187.   **Answer (A) is the correct answer.** The *ad coelom* doctrine says that a landowner's rights extend downward to the center of the earth and upward to the heavens. A number of courts have held that the installation of cable television wires — above or below the ground — are beyond the scope of existing utility easements. An easement would not even be needed, though, if a property owner did not have the right to exclude wires above or below the surface of the land. The fact that the property owner does have such a right to exclude demonstrates that the *ad coelom* doctrine still applies in at least some instances.

Answer (B) is incorrect because the judicial unwillingness to find trespass liability resulting from air pollution depends on the invisible size of the polluting particles, rather than on any understanding about the vertical limit of property ownership. **Answer (C) is**

incorrect because state regulation of groundwater pumping actually demonstrates that landowners do not have an absolute right to any water that is located beneath their land. **Answer (D) is incorrect** because awarding buried treasure to finders is contrary to the ad coelom doctrine's suggestion that a landowner owns everything located under the surface of her land.

188. **Answer (D) is the correct answer.** The general rule is that the sale of property "as is" means that a seller has no duty to disclose information about the premises unless (a) there is a confidential or fiduciary relationship between the parties, or (b) the seller has actively concealed something. A few courts have extended the seller's duty if the seller fails to disclose a condition created by the seller and reasonably knowable to the seller but not the buyer, such as the seller's cultivating the reputation that a house is haunted. Even that rule would not require you to tell Julia about the possible contamination, though, because the seller here did nothing to spread that belief.

Answer (A) is incorrect because there is no obligation to tell a prospective buyer about the absence of a problem with the property. **Answer (B) is incorrect** because there is no obligation to tell the seller about a reputation that the buyer did nothing to create. **Answer (C) is incorrect** because both Answer (A) and Answer (B) are incorrect.

189. **Answer (D) is the correct answer.** Harold did not do anything to establish a property right to the parking space. He merely used it. The condominiums apparently permitted that use, but they were allowed to revoke that permission when they reduced the size of the parking space.

Answer (A) is incorrect because Harold has not offered any evidence that his ownership of a condo unit includes ownership of the parking space. Nor has Harold established adverse possession to the parking space. **Answer (B) is incorrect** because the condominiums did not misrepresent anything to Harold, which is a requirement in most jurisdictions in order to establish an easement by estoppel. **Answer (C) is incorrect** because Harold failed to offer any evidence that he claimed a property right to use the parking space, and the use is presumed to have been with the consent of the condominiums.

190. **Answer (C) is the correct answer.** A number of states have adopted the new Restatement rule, which allows an easement owner to unilaterally relocate an easement under certain circumstances. But most jurisdictions retain the traditional rule, which prohibits such unilateral relocation of an easement. That rule will cause Mr. & Mrs. Gonzalez to lose their lawsuit to relocate the easement.

Answer (A) is incorrect the burden on Anita is irrelevant under the traditional rule, which does not allow unilateral relocation of an easement in any circumstances. **Answer (B) is incorrect** because Mr. & Mrs. Gonzalez appear to believe that they are acting pursuant to their express easement, rather than claiming that they have a new right to cross Anita's land. Even if the use of the new path was under a claim of right that was hostile to Anita's rights, four years will not be enough to establish a prescriptive easement. **Answer (D) is incorrect** because Mr. & Mrs. Gonzalez want to use the easement for its original purpose, which remains within the scope of the original easement.

191. **Answer (D) is the correct answer.** As a result of the property exchange with the city, Nichols now has the fee simple title to his new parcel. There is no evidence that the city

reserved an easement across that land when it conveyed it to Nichols. Accordingly, the city has no right to keep the sewer line there, and its continued presence constitutes a trespass.

Answer (A) is incorrect because the city has not demonstrated that it claims a right to continue to use the land that it no longer owns. Nor has the city used the land contrary to Nichols' ownership for a long enough period to establish an easement by prescription. **Answer (B) is incorrect** because an easement by implication arises only when both the benefitted and burdened properties were originally owned by the same party, and there is no evidence of that here. **Answer (C) is incorrect** because Nichols has the right to exclude others from the area immediately below his land. The precise extent of that subsurface ownership is uncertain, but it undoubtedly extends to the depth at which sewer lines are installed.

192.   **Answer (B) is the correct answer.** Zoning regulations do not automatically render existing uses illegal. Rather, the doctrine of nonconforming uses permits the continuation of a use that existed when the zoning law went into effect. The right to a nonconforming use runs with the land, so Bell may continue to operate a junk yard there just as Cline did before the zoning law was enacted.

Answer (A) is incorrect because Bell is not required to use the property as it is currently zoned — single family residential. Bell simply has to use the property as Cline did before the zoning law went into effect. **Answer (C) is incorrect** because Bell need not continue all of the nonconforming uses that Cline had engaged in on the property before the zoning law was enacted. **Answer (D) is incorrect** because the duration of a nonconforming use varies among jurisdictions. While a few jurisdictions may limit a nonconforming use to 30 years, many other jurisdictions have other — or no — limits on the duration of a nonconforming use.

193.   **Answer (C) is the correct answer.** A city, or any governmental entity, has the general power to purchase property from a willing seller. The city's proposed use of the property to give to its retired mayor may be unwise, but it is not prevented by property law.

Answers (A) and (B) incorrect because the purchase of property to give to the retired mayor may not qualify as a public use, even under the U.S. Supreme Court's decision in *City of New London v. Kelo*, regardless of whether the mayor pays the city back or the city's voters approve it. **Answer (D) is incorrect** because Answer (C) is correct.

194.   **Answer (A) is the correct answer.** RIHR will be able to bring a successful takings claim if the permit condition is judged to be an exaction. The U.S. Supreme Court has held that a permit condition constitutes an exaction unless there is (a) an essential nexus between legitimate state interests and the permit condition, and (b) a rough proportionality between the condition and the projected impact of the proposed development. Requiring RIHR to rebuilding the collapsed wall will fail the rough proportionality test if the wall is located on property owned by someone else because RIHR's actions would be unrelated to the status of the wall.

Answer (B) is incorrect because public use is not one of the factors used to judge an exaction. **Answer (C) is incorrect** because RIHR's knowledge of the collapsed wall is irrelevant to the constitutional test for exactions. **Answer (D) is incorrect** because the city's conditioning the permit on rebuilding the wall satisfies both the essential nexus and rough proportionality tests if the wall is needed to prevent flooding.

195. **Answer (D) is the correct answer.** The federal Telecommunications Act (TCA) does not impose any direct regulation on private land use decisions. Rather, the TCA limits the ability of local zoning law to restrict the location of cell phone towers. RLUIPA operates in the same way: it limits the ability of local zoning officials to restrict the location of churches and other religious land uses.

   Answer (A) is incorrect because the Clean Water Act's wetlands provisions directly regulate private land use decisions. Those provisions operate independently of any local zoning law provisions. **Answer (B) is incorrect** because CERCLA imposes a federal obligation to cleanup hazardous wastes and to pay for those cleanups. Again, CERCLA does not limit local zoning law decisions. **Answer (C) is incorrect** because the ESA directly regulates private land use, too, if it harms the habitat of a listed species. The ESA operates independently of local zoning law.

196. **Answer (C) is the correct answer.** The notion of the public trust presupposes that the people once owned the property in their sovereign capacity. The public trust doctrine then operates to limit uses of the land that conflict with that trust, regardless of whether title to the land is now publicly or privately held.

   A is incorrect because the eminent domain power authorizes the government to buy land or other property, whereas the public trust doctrine applies regardless of who owns the property. Indeed, the government may not need to exercise its eminent domain power if the restriction that it seeks to place upon property use is already contained in the public trust doctrine. Likewise, **B is incorrect** because the public trust doctrine operates independently of the government's acquisition of land, no matter how the property is acquired. **D is incorrect** because the police power provides distinct authority for the government to regulate land use. Land that is subject to a public trust already contains restrictions on land use, so the use of the police power may be unnecessary.

197. **Answer (A) is the correct answer.** Justice Holmes stated the "goes too far" test in *Pennsylvania Coal Co. v. Mahon* (1922), which held that a state statute prohibiting coal mining in such a way as to cause the subsidence of a home works a taking for which the government must exercise its eminent domain power and pay just compensation. In other words, whether or not a government land use regulation "goes too far" determines whether or not that regulation constitutes a regulatory taking requiring just compensation.

   Answer (B) is incorrect because the U.S. Supreme Court has developed a separate test for determining whether the government's conditional approval of a land use permit constitutes an exaction for which just compensation is required. The "goes too far" test does not apply to exactions. **Answer (C) is incorrect** because the Rule against Perpetuities applies to property ownership, not government regulation. **Answer (D) is incorrect** because the express or implied federal preemption of state nuisance law is judged by a distinct jurisprudence that does not feature the "goes too far" test.

198. **Answer (A) is the correct answer.** Intellectual property, including copyrights and trademarks, are subject to the takings clause, so the government must compensate intellectual property owners when it takes their property. Copyright law and trademark law both give the property owner the right to license any — or no — uses of the property. Here the government used the AFA's web site, which could be protected by both copyright and trademark law. Government use of property constitutes a taking without need to consider

any balancing tests or the more generalized equities of the dispute.

B is incorrect because an important public purpose does not eliminate the requirement that the government pay for the property that it takes. The congressional purpose will provide evidence that the public use test is satisfied, but just compensation is still due. **C is incorrect** because web site designs are property — they may be copyrighted, they may employ protected trademarks, and they may even contain patented features (though there is no evidence of that in this case). **D is incorrect** because government use of property constitutes a taking, even if the property owner has suffered a very minor loss. In *Loretto v. Teleprompter Manhattan CATV Corp.*, 458 U.S. 419 (1982), for example, the Supreme Court held that a taking occurred when the city used an apartment building for the location of a cable television box, even though the resulting compensation was determined to be just one dollar.

199. **Answer (A) is the correct answer.** In regulatory takings law, the denominator problem refers to the difficulty in identifying the specific property that is affected by the city's regulation. Alicia will argue that the city has taken all three of its remaining acres, or 100% of her remaining land, which qualifies as a total taking for which compensation is due. The city, by contrast, will insist that the regulation has affected only three of Alicia's twenty acres, or 15% of her land, which falls far short of a total taking and is thus subject to the more flexible balancing test. In each instance, the numerator is the same — three — but the opposing denominators of three and twenty account for the radically different calculations of the fraction of the land that the city's regulation affects.

B is incorrect because there is no dispute about the amount of land affected by the state's wetlands regulation — all 50 acres are affected. Whether or not the wetlands work a taking is uncertain, but that question is distinct from the denominator problem. **C is incorrect** because the city's exercise of its eminent domain power may raise questions concerning the motivation of the city in taking land from a religious organization, but that does not implicate the denominator problem. **D is incorrect** because it describes an exaction, which raises a distinct takings issue from the denominator problem as well. The courts will analyze the constitutionality of the city's exaction by considering the nexus and proportionality to the city's interests, rather than engaging in the judgment about the fraction of the property affected in order to resolve the denominator problem.

200. Answer (D) is the correct answer. The express easement between Rob and Jerry extended to "ingress and egress to Jerry's property." The scope of that easement, therefore, does not encompass a right to vegetation, so **A is incorrect**. Jerry cannot claim a prescriptive easement that entitles him to keep the trees, either, because there is no indication that Jerry planted and cared for the trees under a claim of right. Jerry may have thought he had a legal right to plant the trees, but he may have simply wanted to beautify the area provided that Rob did not object. The burden is on Jerry to establish a prescriptive easement, and the uncertainty will operate against him. Thus **B and C are incorrect**, too.

201. **Answer (B) is the correct answer.** An easement by necessity arises only in circumstances when the dominant and servient tenement was once owned by the same person. Dawn's only options are to obtain an express easement or try to establish an easement by estoppel or an easement by prescription, but nothing in the facts suggests that she will satisfy the criteria for those two kinds of implied easements.

A is incorrect because the failure to obtain an easement by the agreement of the landowner does not prejudice any claims that an implied easement has been established. **C is incorrect** because it was not necessary to cross Jim's land when Patricia divided it; the fact that the traffic bothered Patricia will qualify as an annoyance, but not a necessity. **D is incorrect** because the expense and difficulty that would attend Dawn's building such a road could persuade courts in some jurisdictions that it is practically impossible to leave Dawn's property in that manner, and therefore, crossing Jim's road is necessary.

202. **Answer (C) is the correct answer.** State right-to-farm statutes protect farmers from nuisance liability, and thus they afford a property right to farmers to engage in farming activities regardless of their effects. A neighbor who objects to the farm's activities will have to negotiate with the farm to surrender that property right rather than suing to hold the farm liable.

    A and B are incorrect because the farms protected by right-to-farm statutes are potential defendants, not plaintiffs. **D is incorrect** because the statutes give farms a property right to engage in farming activities, not a right to hold those who interfere with such activities liable.

203. **Answer (C) is the correct answer.** Celia is a mistaken improver. She did not intentionally trespass in order to obtain the grapes. She then transformed the grapes into something far more valuable. That transformation caused the original grapes to become a different species, so Celia will be able to keep everything except that she will have to reimburse her neighbor for the original value of the grapes.

    A is incorrect because the meteorite that Anna took belonged to her neighbor by virtue of the ownership of the land on which it fell, and Anna was an intentional trespasser onto her neighbor's land. **B is incorrect** because Betty was an intentional trespasser and thus outside the rules protecting "mistaken" improvers. **C is incorrect** because Daphne worked only an insignificant improvement in the value of the turtle shell, so her neighbor will be entitled to get it back.

204. **Answer (D) is the correct answer.** David cannot point to any legal rule that will excuse him from paying rent. Commercial premises are rarely covered by an implied warranty of habitability. David might be able to establish a constructive eviction, but he will have to leave the premises if he wants to stop paying rent. The noise might constitute a nuisance, but the existence of a nuisance provides an independent cause of action for damages that does not excuse the affected tenant from his duty to pay rent.

    A is incorrect because most states prohibit a landlord from taking any action in retaliation for a tenant asserting his or her rights. **B is incorrect** because there is no evidence that the lease between Bryce and Boyd prohibited Boyd from subleasing the farmland. Courts presume that land is freely alienable unless the parties state otherwise. **C is incorrect** because the failure to provide water to a residential property will violate the implied warranty of habitability that exists in nearly every state. That warranty cannot be waived, and a tenant is allowed to not pay rent but stay in possession if it is violated.

205. **Answer (A) is the correct answer.** Single-family homes that are sold or rented by their owner are exempt from the Fair Housing Act, provided that the owner does not use a realtor or own more than three rental properties. Thus, a homeowner can discriminate based upon

race or any other protected characteristic as far as the FHA is concerned.

B is incorrect because the FHA does not allow a benevolent motive to excuse decisions based upon race or any other protected characteristic. **C is incorrect** because the FHA covers advertising for housing as well as the actual sale and rental of housing. **D is incorrect** because the FHA prohibits discrimination based upon religion, again notwithstanding any desire to create a particular kind of community.

206.   **Answer (A) is the correct answer.** Although they discussed ending their marriage, George and Syliva still owned the house as tenants by the entirety when Sylvia died. A tenancy by the entirety, like a joint tenancy, includes a right of survivorship. Thus, George obtained Sylvia's interest when she died, so George owns the house in fee simple absolute.

   Answer (B) is incorrect because Sylvia's interest in the house passed to George when Sylvia died, so Betsy did not acquire any interest in the housed from Sylvia's will. **Answer (C) is incorrect** because George obtained Sylvia's interest via the right of survivorship. **Answer (D) is incorrect** because Sylvia's death ended the tenancy by the entirety, rather than converting it into a joint tenancy.

207.   **Answer (D) is the correct answer.** Slightly more than half community property states mandate an equal distribution of marital assets, not an equitable distribution. The mutual fund containing the savings from their income is a marital asset because Melinda and Brandon acquired it while they were married. By contrast, the car was a gift to Brandon alone, and such individualized gifts are treated as separate property, not marital property.

   A is incorrect both because Melinda is not entitled to the car and because a minority of community property states require an equitable distribution of marital property. **B is incorrect** because Melinda is most likely entitled to an equal distribution, or perhaps an equitable distribution, of the mutual fund. **C is incorrect** because Melinda is not entitled to any part of the value of the car.

208.   **Answer (D) is the correct answer.** Gerald's conveyance of his interest in the vacation home did not terminate the tenancy by the entirety because only mutual consent, death, or divorce can do that. Gerald was free, however, to convey his interest in the land, but it retained its status as a tenancy by the entirety with Alice. Upon Gerald's death, Alice took the whole property by operation of the right of survivorship inherent in the tenancy by the entirety. Gerald's creditors, by contrast, got nothing. They would have obtained the whole property, though, if Alice had died before Gerald. That did not happen, though, so **answers (A), (B), and (C) are all incorrect** because they wrongly indicate that Gerald's creditors have a property interest in the vacation home.

209.   **Answer (B) is the correct answer.** A partition action is available whenever two or more tenants in common are unable to agree about the appropriate use, or disposition, of their property. The fact that Joseph has lived there since before Kelly obtained an interest in the property will not allow Joseph to defeat Kelly's legitimate interests as a tenant in common.

   A is incorrect because tenants in common hold equal rights, regardless of whether they are in possession of the property or not. **C is incorrect** because a tenancy in common can be conveyed without destroying the interest, so Joseph did not obtain the land in fee when Frank sold it. **D is incorrect** because Joseph cannot block a partition action simply by paying rent to Kelly. Joseph may persuade Kelly not to seek a partition, or Kelly may be entitled to rent in limited circumstances, but Kelly will always retain the right to seek a partition sale of the house if he chooses to do so.

210. **Answer (B) is the correct answer.** The conveyance from Axle gave Lucy a life estate and Annie a vested remainder. That remainder was vested because Lucy's "eldest daughter" was ascertainable as Lucy at the time of the conveyance from Axle. Upon Lucy's death, Annie's remainder became possessory. But Annie had conveyed that remainder to the Prairie Land Trust, which now holds the land in fee simple.

A is incorrect because Axle did not retain any property interest once it conveyed the riverfront property. **C is incorrect** because Tanya was not Lucy's "eldest daughter." It is possible that "her eldest daughter" could be interpreted to mean the oldest daughter of Lucy's who was living at the time of Lucy's death, but the better interpretation construes "her eldest daughter" at the time of the conveyance. **D is incorrect** because Lucy could not convey a greater interest in the property than she owned herself. Dean Walter thus entered into the five-year lease with the risk that Lucy would not live five more years, and thus her interest in the land would end.

211. **Answer (B) is the correct answer.** Jane's attempt to convey a tenancy by the entirety to Julie and Henry failed because you cannot own property in a tenancy by the entirety if you are not married. The fact that Julie and Henry got married two years later does not change the status of the estate that Jane conveyed — and thus **A is incorrect**. An unsuccessful effort to create a tenancy by the entirety will either result in a joint tenancy or a tenancy in common, with different jurisdictions reaching different conclusions. **D is incorrect** because Jane gave Julie an executory interest if she and Henry ever got divorced, not a contingent remainder. **C is incorrect** because that executory interest is shifting, not springing, because it would divest a transferee instead of Jane. The shifting executory interest satisfies the Rule against Perpetuities using either Julie or Henry as the measuring life.

212. **Answer (A) is the correct answer.** Mountain Realty conveyed a life estate to Elaine while keeping the reversion for itself. Regardless of how Elaine conveyed her interest, the property was always destined to return to Mountain Realty upon her death.

B is incorrect both because Elaine was incapable of devising her life estate in the 10 acres of land, and even if she had been allowed to do so, Randy attempted to convey his interest to Sara. **C is incorrect** because she obtained the land from Randy, who did not own any interest that he could convey. **D is incorrect** because the county did obtain the 10 acres from Elaine, but only for the duration of Elaine's life. When Elaine died, her life estate ended, and the county's interest in the land ended, too.

213. **A is the correct answer.** The copyright law does apply to live performances. But Mattel does not own a copyright in "Barbie"; it owns a trademark. Aqua is thus potentially liable for trademark infringement, but not copyright infringement.

B is incorrect because parodies of copyrighted works are permitted, provided that they do not create a likelihood of confusion about the source of the parody. Here the fact that the song does not imply that it was created by Mattel eliminates the likelihood of confusion. **C is incorrect** because it, too, will explain why Mattel will lose: the first amendment does protect a song that is not purely commercial speech. Finally, the song does satisfy the noncommercial use exception which is contained in the Federal Trademark Dilution Act, and thus **D is incorrect.**

214.   **Answer (C) is the correct answer.** To date, and despite numerous proposals and many scholarly suggestions, commercial sperm banks have been subjected to relatively little government regulation. Most states have thus far been unwilling to approve more extensive regulations of such operations. Their unwillingness to do so, however, is unrelated to the other three answers.

    A is incorrect because human body parts are treated as property in a number of instances, though certainly not all of them. **B is incorrect** because the constitutional limits upon state regulation of human reproduction do not prevent all such regulation. A state may regulate when it has a compelling state interest to do so, or perhaps when it assures that the affected parties will not suffer an undue burden. **D is incorrect** because the agreements between commercial sperm banks and donors have been inadequate on a number of instances, yet the appropriate governmental response has yet to be determined.

215.   **Answer (B) is the correct answer.** The fair use provision is a statutory exception to the general provisions of the copyright act that afford writers and other copyright holders a limited monopoly to their works. Fair use recognizes the public's interest in access to written works even while they are protected by copyright law, and the concomitant need to limit the monopoly that the statute grants to copyright holders. The precise scope of the fair use provision remains controversial, especially as technology greatly aids both copyright holders and those desiring to use copyrighted works without having to obtain permission.

    A is incorrect because the nature of ideas as property or not is unrelated to the justifications for the fair use exception. **C is incorrect** because natural rights claims are unlikely to be successful in the context of copyrights, even when asserted by the creators themselves. **D is incorrect** because many commercial works in fact remain valuable for many years or generations, as the recent controversy over the copyrights held by the Walt Disney Company illustrates.

216.   **Answer (C) is the correct answer.** Omar purchased the pen from Samuel the day before Kelly took it from the display case. Unlike a gift, the sale of personal goods does not require their delivery to transfer ownership. Samuel's acceptance of Omar's check created a contract that entitled Omar to the pen.

    A is incorrect because Samuel has accepted Omar's money and provided a written document conveying title to the pen. **B is incorrect** because Samuel did not deliver the pen to Kelly. The fact that Kelly came into possession of the pen does not establish that Samuel delivered it to him. **D is incorrect** because nothing indicates that Jefferson's heirs had an ownership interest in the pen, and Jefferson or his descendants could have conveyed the pen to another party at any time.

217.   **Answer (C) is the correct answer.** Jeff voluntarily gave the laptop to We Fix It, thus giving the store voidable title to the laptop. Voidable title, in turn, can be conveyed to a good faith purchaser. Monica had no reason to know that the laptop was Jeff's when she bought it from the store, so she qualifies as a good faith purchaser. The fact that she later discovered the mistake does not eliminate that status as a good faith purchaser, either.

    A and B are incorrect because a bona fide purchaser gains better title than the original owner. **D is incorrect** because We Fix It acquired voidable title, not void title, when Jeff voluntarily gave the laptop to the store. The store would have received void title only if it had taken the computer without his knowledge and consent.

218. **Answer (C) is the correct answer.** This problem is based upon *Basket v. Hassell*, 107 U.S. 602 (1882). Chaney attempted to grant Martin a gift causa mortis. But the death of the donor cannot be a precondition to the validity of a gift causa mortis because such a condition indicates a lack of a present intent to give the gift.

A is incorrect because the lack of Chaney's present intent to give the certificate of deposit to Martin prevents the transaction from qualifying as a valid gift causa mortis. B and D are incorrect because while delivery of the gift was accomplished, the intent to give the certificate was lacking.

219. **Answer (B) is the correct answer.** Most courts hold that the bank's acceptance of Julia's antique watch created a bailment. The loss of the watch while it was within the bank's control would constitute negligence for which the bank would be liable to Julia.

A is incorrect because most courts hold that a bailment is not created when landowners allow another person to park a car on their land. An absence of guards or other means of physical control will further support the conclusion that there has not been a bailment. **C is incorrect** because while a bailment was created, a bailor will not be held liable for the loss of very valuable goods that the bailor had no reason to expect where entrusted to its care. **D is incorrect** there is no indication that the department store took control over the purse, and until it does, no bailment is created.

220. **Answer (A) is the correct answer.** Like any other interest in land, a tenancy at will can be created orally if it is for a duration of less than one year. Interests in land for more than one year are subject to the Statute of Frauds, which requires that their creation be in writing.

B is incorrect because a real covenant must be in writing to be enforceable. Indeed, a reciprocal negative easement is the only example of a covenant that can be implied rather than be in writing. **C is incorrect** because a homeowner's association's recreational fee is simply a type of covenant that is governed by the same rule which explains why B is incorrect. **D is incorrect** because all zoning provisions — like every other legislative act — must be in writing.

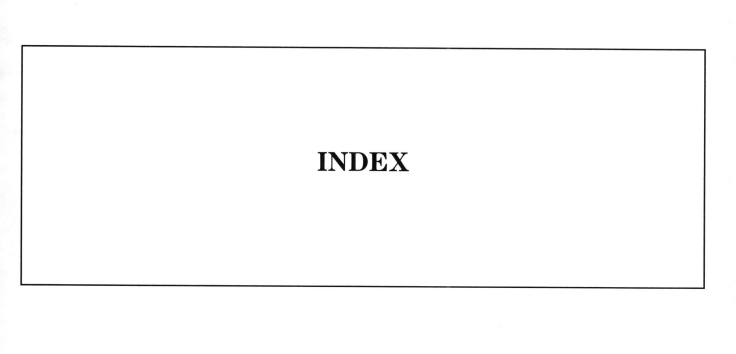

INDEX

INDEX